In a different light

In a different light

Fourteen contemporary dutch-language poets

Edited by rob schouten & robert minhinnick

seren

Seren is the book imprint of
Poetry Wales Press Ltd
Nolton Street, Bridgend, Wales
www.seren-books.com

ISBN 1-85411-313-5

A CIP record for this title is available from
the British Library

*The publisher works with the financial assistance of the
Arts Council of Wales*

*This book was published with the financial assistance of
the Foundation for the Production and Translation of Dutch Literature*

Cover photograph by Helen Sweeting, 'Blue Changing Room', from the series
'Abandoned Lidos and Forgotten Pools'.

Printed in Plantin by Bell & Bain, Glasgow

CONTENTS

H.H. TER BALKT
translated by Lloyd Haft

ANNA ENQUIST
translated by Lloyd Haft

LEONARD NOLENS
translated by Paul Vincent

K. MICHEL
translated by William Groenewegen

INTRODUCTION

THE NETHERLANDS lies in a delta, which through the course of the centuries, has been ploughed and cultivated by the inhabitants into an important harbour and trading area, which in some respects can be called the gateway to the European continent. A delta is, geographically speaking, flat land and perhaps this is also valid in social terms. Great disparities have been ironed out: everyone is equal. This principle of equality, which was further promoted by numerous voyages of discovery and trading expeditions from the Netherlands, and which gave the small country an open-minded, world-centred outlook, fostered not only one of the first western European democracies after the Greek city states, but also a culture that enriches itself with everything that comes its way; the country is a sponge and the Dutch are beachcombers.

Being only a small country, with a population of fourteen million, the Netherlands has evidently been subject to a great deal of foreign influence. Of old, many foreigners crossed its borders on account of the tolerant climate. In the seventeenth 'Golden Century', the Netherlands became a free port for foreign dissidents who were not able to survive at home, and the Netherlands still teems with uprooted influences. If there is one thing characteristic of the Netherlands, then it is the high level of globalisation. These things are clearly to be observed in the culture, and therefore in the poetry too.

The Dutch arts have never been particularly nationalistic; this is something they simply could not countenance. Dutch literary art fits seamlessly into the far greater history of Western literature. One encounters equivalents for all of the great movements in Dutch poetry – Romanticism, Modernism and Post-Modernism, but they are seldom coloured in a specifically Dutch way; though this in itself is perhaps a typical characteristic of Dutch culture. It is not the sort of country that

11

is given to great political and national commotion, and what has taken place has largely remained buried beneath the poetical surface. There is, then, little engaged poetry. One finds barely any perceptible trace of the greatest event of the previous century, the Second World War. In post-war history too, which in the turbulent 1960's led to a spectacular rapprochement through the demolition of the old ideological pillars of Protestantism, Catholicism and socialism, one finds no poetical echo. A typical national news item that tended to make the international broadcasts in the 1970's – the Moluccan train hijackings – did not inspire poetic contemplation. And of the ultra-liberal spirit that illumines the Netherlands too, where abortion and euthanasia are regulated by law, where homosexuals can marry, and where you can see soft-porn on your TV every evening, you see no thematic reflection in the poetry. Dutch poetry of the last century has been internally directed and intimate, or else wholly outwardly directed and universal. This is equally true of the post-war poems collected in this anthology.

The cultural impasse within which the country found itself after 1945 led, in the 1950's, to one of the most interesting movements in Dutch poetry from the previous century, the so-called Fifties' movement. Just as in the rest of Europe, a war (the First World War) was necessary to get Modernism going, this was also the case in the Netherlands (which had remained neutral from 1914-1918). The Fifties' poets were the Dutch answer to European Modernism. A movement developed in opposition to traditional romantic-realistic poetry, which saw the poem not as the vehicle for communiqués, but as an organism; language was no longer an instrument for communication, but material, as paint is for the artist. These Fifties' poets influenced Dutch poetry profoundly, and part of that influence stems from the fact that they were to provoke a counter-reaction. Various poets, such as Gerrit Kouwenaar and Remco Campert, were directly associated with the movement, but its influence is also to be detected in the poetry of H. H. ter Balkt. Perhaps Kouwenaar has remained the most consistent executor of the Fifties' ideal; other poets, such as Campert, would ultimately arrive at a more accessible and urbane conversational tone, which was never very distant in Dutch post-war poetry.

The poetry of the Fifties' produced lyrical highpoints, but also occasional hermetic linguistic constructions, which clearly excluded a large number of readers. A reaction was inevitable. In the 1960's, this would take the form of Neo-Realism: writers and poets attempted to engage with the real world as if it were something new: the surprising nature of the everyday and the overly-accepted became common topics. Alongside poets who were occupied with material reality in the line of the old Dadaists, and fabricated ready-mades, other categories of poets also emerged, who were primarily concerned with everyday psychological reality. This is a form of poetry that has always been prevalent in the Netherlands, and is closely connected to the Christian-Humanist origins of Dutch culture. From the pre-war period until the present day, poets have been interested in the psychological and social realities of their fellow man. In the poems of Hans R. Vlek, Rutger Kopland and Judith Herzberg, all thoughts of higher symbolic pretensions have been removed. These poets are concerned with simple, direct, universal humanity. The poem 'Young Lettuce' by Rutger Kopland: 'I can take it all,/ the withering of beans,/ flowers dying... But young lettuce in September... in moist little beds, no.' was to become something of a classic. Whoever reads it must consider that it was written in a time when the Netherlands had been turned on its head culturally and socially; hippies and provos trumpeted social re-unification; the old prevailing social order was swept away, but in the poetry there is no sign to be found.

Poetry preferred to depict doubt-ridden, somewhat worrisome Twentieth Century man. It is a predilection that is to be seen again in later poets such as J. Eijkelboom, Eva Gerlach and Anna Enquist; their perspective is determined by the solitary individual in awkward contact with the outside world. A striking feature is the absence of flamboyant feminist or emancipatory qualities in the work of the best-known female poets of this period. In the case of Willem van Toorn though, who is akin to the psychological-realistic poets, you still see a residue of the old Fifties' ideal. For him, poetry remains a mechanism that creates its own reality.

A great deal of the poetry in the Netherlands of the 1970's was concerned with such topics as death, stillness, and minute alterations of perspective. In the middle of the 1980's, a generation of young Dutch poets had seen enough of what they considered to be a sterile poetical climate. What is currently known worldwide as Post-Modernism initially manifested itself in a rebellious movement called the Maximums. After initial resistance had subsided, it became clear that the primary survivors were poets who looked upon the world with a powerful and sometimes baroque amazement. K. Michel and Esther Jansma are striking examples of this; there is little to be found in their work of the reticent nature of much post-war Dutch poetry. They take reality and fantasy firmly by the hand.

This had been the case for many years in Flemish poetry, which had always remained closer to the old Fifties' ideal. The grand old man of the entire Dutch-language tradition, Hugo Claus, has continued to write moving and baroque poetry, and this is equally true of Leonard Nolens, for whom the great human conditions of death, love and alienation have continued to provide the inspiration for an equally personal and passionate verse.

With its universal cosmopolitanism, the Dutch poetry of the last five decades has proven to be extremely fruitful ground. This is not only true for the homegrown poets, but also for the great foreigners, whose work has been made accessible through countless translations. It is not by chance that the Netherlands is a country of festivals, such as the famous Poetry International, illustrating the warm-hearted, open character of Dutch poetry. This anthology will give the reader the opportunity to enjoy the rich and vital character of poetry composed on this small sponge on the North Sea. This anthology could have looked quite different because every selection is a matter of personal choice. It may have included work by the great Fifties' poet Lucebert, the linguistic monuments of Kees Ouwens, and Hans Faverey's poems permeated with Zen mysticism, or else the inimitable linguistic dexterity of Leo Vroman, or the innovative classicism of Gerrit Komrij, the present Poet Laureate. I do not name by chance poets who, because of their idiosyncratic use of language, are scarcely translatable. We have included important poets whose poetry also works well in translation, so that the reader can appreciate its rich aroma.

Lastly, this anthology is the sister volume to *In een ander licht – Contemporary Poetry from Wales*. As with that anthology, a great deal of sifting work and organisation of translations was carried out by P.C. Evans and Robert Minhinnick. Without their contribution, this book would never have been published.

ROB SCHOUTEN, Amsterdam, 2001

trans. P.C. EVANS

AMAZED IN THE LABYRINTH

MY CO-EDITOR, Rob Schouten, underlines that this selection of poems lacks engagement with the political. Considering it spans the second half of the last century, that is a surprising fact. And certainly the absence of reference to World War II is startling. Of course, the images are there: from Eijkelboom, Vlek, Kopland and others. But there is no rawness in the reference. Already the death-camps, the war-weariness, the ineffable blight have been tucked into history's filing cabinet.

> I trace the windows of the barrack huts,
> watch-towers, gas-chamber.
>
> Only the black reflection of distance
> in the panes, of a peaceful landscape,
>
> and beyond it, no-one.
>
> (Rutger Kopland, 'Natzweiler' trans. James Brockway)

Few poets would argue that there are things that cannot be written. Yet perhaps poetry is not the medium for the Low Countries' war experience. There is no-one here remotely like Paul Celan (though no other writer could possibly be like Celan) who might have taken on the themes of disappearance, fragmentation, stark horror. There is none of Celan's "black milk of morning" in this collection. But no verse squeezing itself into appalled and ultimate silence either.

So, life triumphs. As it must. The poets look at the peace. At lifestyle, leisure, the feud with futility. Again, surprisingly, there is little poetry of *things*. Particularities do not exercise these writers as they do those in the English-speaking world. Moods, ideas, even philosophies are dealt with instead. However, there is an idiosyncratic 'nature' poetry here. Typically it is a regulated nature. The poets commiserate with what natural remnants survive for the tidiness man has imposed in his draughtsman's regime. Thus the pylons hum, the polder gleams, and the sky overflows into the eyes of the artists, that immense marine sky, Gerrit Kouwenaar's 'high dilapidated blue of a sky', its cloud shadows hastening over the farm-dotted pelt of the Low Countries.

For light also is a constant if ungraspable subject. But is it light or humanity itself that Kouwenaar depicts as 'amazed in the labyrinth'? As to the wild, there are few other creatures to make man doubt his supremacy. Anna Enquist's hare surprises us by the very fact of its existence. What is it doing? The hare is all that remains – and a timorous remnant it is – of a possible elemental past whose savagery, at least in the British Isles, might yet extrude into the present. But there's no possibility of that in the Low Countries. No iron-fearing fairytale denizens there, no Celtic-Roman-Saxon-Viking substrata for a David Jones or Ted Hughes or Seamus Heaney to excavate. The writers of *In a Different Light* have rid themselves of myth. Of threat, it seems there is only the sea, waiting, electrified, with its pylon voices. The paganisms these poets confront come dressed by the modern world. And are all the more terrifying for that.

Considering that this book appears from a Welsh publisher, I asked myself what the people of the Low Countries might know of Wales. Rumours of mountains, seas and language? Wales is small compared to Belgium and The Netherlands. It lacks their succulent humus of money, their prismatic global vision of themselves, their thriving cosmopolitanism with its constant infusions of new blood and ideas. Wales must make do with peripherality. Too much of it is a margin within a margin. As yet, it is no-one's idea of a European country.

Now there is nothing intrinsically wrong with this. It brings a lonely strength. Yet in terms of cosmopolitanism, Wales cannot even build literary bridges between its own two languages. And apart from Amsterdam's Cassa Rossa and the gulleys and ginnels of the Walletjes, what do we know of the Low Countries? Too few of us have experienced the festivals of Rotterdam, the civilised pace of towns such as Dordrecht, the melding that money brings between the medieval and the modern within the cities of Belgium. We remain strangers to that sense of easy integration and effortless identity that comes from being at the heart of Europe.

So what characterises this poetry? Above all, its intelligence: that territory between the playful and the cerebral. There is little description here. If there is confrontation it is minor and soon moves to other matters. Yes, there is literalism, but never an avoidance of richer, stranger possibilities. Most often the poetry is in the implicit, for these poets, different as they are, share it seems a scorn for the explicit, a scorn for, yes, description for its own sake. The Anglo-Welsh writer, Raymond Garlick, wrote many of his poems in 'Holland', and memorably found "A people at grips / With genesis / Not apocalypse."[1] Certainly Garlick idealised The Netherlands and used it as a measuring-stick against his own adopted country.

Yet Garlick's Dutch poems are almost all descriptive, and too often deliver a poem-crushing moral in the last verse. Garlick was little influenced by the 'experimentalists' who were at work when he lectured in the country. A pinch of that Dutch confidence, its risk-taking, for example, would have allowed European fresh air into his severely formal and self-restrictive verses. However, one Welsh-linked writer who would seem to have taken some Dutch lessons to heart, is Jeremy Hooker. As to other literary versions of the Low Countries, Irvine Welsh's Amsterdam is a parody of a parody. But there is always Ian McEwan, while perhaps the most evocative conjuring in recent English fiction is Alan Hollinghurst's *The Folding Star*.

For the poets in this volume, description, their rule states, is where writing might be permitted to begin. But it can never finish there. And in that respect, how alien these poets are to most of the English language writers of Wales. *In a Different Light* shows us as much of the topography of the intellect as it does the plains between Ostend and Groningen. No agonies here of those who strive to win or lose a national identity. Being human is as much as can be accommodated. The tribal, self-lacerating literary debates that occurred in Wales in recent decades, with their emphasis on definition, their trainspotterish attention to who might be included in, or excluded from, a notional national pantheon, would seem primitive in the Netherlands. (As they have done in the rest of the UK).

It's *time* this poetry addresses: "the mass murderer", as Anna Enquist would have it.

All that we know, what we are like,
disappears like wind over the fields.

It's a heroic subject. But concealed by the mundane. In the rollicking 'Ostend', Hugo Claus identifies where life started to decay. Judith Herzberg's wry monologues extract Russian doll from Russian doll, as the minutes pass and her bus fails to arrive. How well these would work in English on radio or from the intimate stage. There's immense good humour in such pieces. Yet even the energy of 'Ostend' cannot disguise the sound of whistling in the dark. Inevitably, Enquist cries out at the injustice of it, even as she admits the impossibility of justice:

> River, flow backwards. Stone,
> be fire again. Air around me,
> be body that carries me and
> comforts. Memory, come undone.

> ('I am poured out like water', trans. Lloyd Haft)

Above all, it is Rutger Kopland who confronts our haemorrhage of days. Kopland with his deceptive conversational veracities is a poet who comprehends the imperishability of small wisdoms. Nevertheless, he places above these the importance of curiosity. Without curiosity, Kopland knows, the mind rots. It will rot anyway, and memory too soon come undone, but while he has the opportunity, Kopland will maintain his questioning of time. All around him the evidence builds. His father, the plover, the fairground. Even the life of light itself. They all tell him what he cannot deny. But although the answers are clear, it's the questions that count, the questions dwarfing the answers, as the heartbreaking banalities of 'Johnson Brothers Ltd' testify.

Poets, we might say, are the pathfinders of language. They are the scouts ahead of the novelists, the playwrights, the benighted waggon-hugging journalists. They find the untrodden ways. Poets discover ecstasy, imagism, confessionalism, they crane towards surrealism's fishy rose. Which means that too often they are absent when the camp fires are built. Translators, I suppose, follow after the poets when the trails are almost cold. In choosing this collection, I was entirely dependent upon translation. And I am the first to admit that this selection of poets might have been significantly different if other translations had been available. Thus there is no Leo Vroman, no Lucebert, no Gerrit Komrij. Their absence here is of course no judgement on their work.

Nethertheless, the reader is invited to delight in the mischievous and mysterious which intertwine in these pages, to enjoy the risky excitement of poets such as H.H. ter Balkt and Leonard Nolens, the urbanity of Willem van Toorn, the wonderful meditations of, not least, Anna Enquist, Eva Gerlach and Esther Jansma, as they teach us how to think, and to think differently. There are difficulties here – and we should be thankful for that – just as there are marvels. They are inextricably linked. Now let us enjoy them all.

It has been my double privilege to edit this book and also to learn from these fourteen poets. I cannot thank them enough.

Finally, I acknowledge the contributions of the translators, the Foundation for the Production and Translation of Dutch Literature, Amsterdam's *Vertalershuis*, and especially those of Rob Schouten, P.C. Evans and Sascha van der Aa, without whom this book would not have been published.

ROBERT MINHINNICK, Porthcawl, Wales, 2002

[1] 'Note on the Iliad' from Raymond Garlick's *Collected Poems*, Gomer, 1987

GERRIT KOUWENAAR

In the nothing between two shell craters
while the grimy slosh of coffee flasks
slows time for a moment

passers-by project their rose memories
on the unhurried air of autumn
like Sunday painters

behind portieres and palm trees
the ghosts of stage comedians dispute
mortality

powdery white lungs immortalize
Wagner, make it reichswehr

carnivorous flowers smirking in vases
of lace donate their future
to the iron labourers on parade

but like a featherbed
bobbing on water in the cellar
the present tense of the past heaves
on the becalmed flesh of the moment

hence the hammers
dismantling remembered heat
into flakes of winter

trans. Lloyd Haft

There's something desperate in the bushes, a sound
as if eating whetted a blade of its own

while the river passes, the eye still
standing, the shore lingering

nearly already remembered the journey, the way one lags
lost in the bed of a child

how the light that changes all things' beds
breaks the seals and festers
amazed in the labyrinth

winter stands still

Write winter stands still, read a day without death
spell the snow like a child, melt time
like a clock trying to see itself in ice

it's ice-cold today, so translate what one writes
into a clock that won't run, into flesh
that's there like snow in the sun

and write how her body was there and bent
supple in flesh and looked back
straight in the eye of today, and read what this says

the sun on the snow, the child in the sled
the track snowed under, illegible death –

trans. Lloyd Haft

the last days of summer

Slower the wasps, scarcer the gadflies
greenflies greyer, angels none, nothing
that heavens here, all burning lower

these are the last days, one writes
the last halt of summer, the last
flames of the year, of the years

what was keeps being there barely
and what one clearly sees has a black border

one must sign off here, imply
the garden in the garden, spare the open book
the ending, withhold oneself

keep secret how language comes caving in at the lips
how the ground swamps the poem, no mouth
shall speak what winters here –

trans. Lloyd Haft

time's still open

Time's still open, there's wheezing at both ends
like evening and darkness embracing, sleeping
till the hoary orchard cracks, pregnant
with flawed fruits gallnuts worms

in the house breath, dates moaning
that the nightshade hangs by its life
that the sower sprouts in his cot
that the green words go bad like cherries

flashes of today, the questions, sighing
of the low once-only trees for a long total
merciful summer, for fall, for winter –

trans. Lloyd Haft

1890: 27-29 July

It didn't work, one walks the road back, running
down like a clock, and shall today lay

upon the bed what's oozing, a straitjacket around
a blood vessel, not much throbs, one had expected

it to liberate, cleanse, spirit
clarified in void, form of bread

but nothing, just that colour, red as a doornail, decay
that kept returning home, dead end

one leaves the room with oneself, one is
myself, above it crows, paint –

a winter evening

Sat a good while watching the cankered stem
of the old elder burning

beyond telling this slow self-absorbed farewell
this birth of ash that goes without saying

and not to be rhymed how meanwhile next to time
in a neighbouring snowed-under now
the dormouse awoke and the radio
was singing the song of the sparkling chalice

and later the white room was blacker and later
than ever and the light-giving watch
held its breath, listening to
the deathless tick of the termite –

trans. Lloyd Haft

So clear it really seldom is, one sees
reeds facing the distance in white

somebody knocks, asks for water, it's
a lost hunter

you can drink the answer, lay it out
in language on its curving way

in his game bag's a pool of blood, the water
slips on the talking tongue till it's wine

look, he says, pointing around the reeds as a way
of bye-bye, this is a robe of mourning

later his glass is still there, one sees
the reeds, has a bite to eat

trans. Lloyd Haft

illegible

Teeming standstill, white, why,
how deep must one see this to ground oneself, dig

to be here and now, future that wanted flesh
and got it wrong, dug-up shovel

sickle and stonesquare practically rooted, echo
chewed over by teeth that always, no words

other than this the intended, gadfly spring sedge
bloodpeach chokepear nightingales, perfect

on this paper that's now getting rained on, now
blowing dry again, date, rest illegible –

trans. Lloyd Haft

Friends, the way we sat there that summer
on that packed mountain between empty graves

the way we sat there frozen in a heat
for one blue second, withdrawn for a later

and the way the cicadas spoke for the gods
ten thousand wings as if they were there

and the way the things grew self-absorbed
gods and dead men eggshells shards

and the way it's autumn now and us still sitting there
like we will when we're away in shards –

trans. Lloyd Haft

trees/grass/mountains

And it's the trees, too: or rather
their presence you feel in the night outside
and us being a century ahead: all those years
of locked-up shutters and darkness, eyes
evaporating in skin

And it's the grass, too, when the snow
is warming beetles and freezing crickets
and me like a haystack in winter
the blaze of a hostel in summer: oh that sweet
high dilapidated blue of a sky while my
hand freezes over a dead name

And it's the mountains, too: their content
unfolds their form so fully: and us
breeding flesh where such a lot of stone is: and
building and breaking far ahead of our senses, seeing
and hearing, feeling and speaking: there's
a wind coming up, a dead tortoise
blocking the road –

trans. Lloyd Haft

this never-ending reprieve

This never-ending reprieve,
this rushed laying up
of evasions, sown rooted harvested

one walks across the last of the fleshy fields,
drooling still from a sumptuous winter

while the sun goes down the house ends up
lost, one stays put though wanting to move

one dreams the infinite table, ground
covers the plates, the kitchen cupboard
gapes like a hole in ice

trans. Lloyd Haft

J. EIJKELBOOM

Sound

I

For words
meanings are too multifarious,
they merely sink
beneath oceans of sound.

The composer trawls his tones out
but he listens to much more.
Finally, fortissimo, cried Mahler,
at Niagara.

But who has understood this?
He who wrote it down
so that it continues to live:
the recorded word
and the spoken word
are not entirely superfluous –
this you shall never
hear me say.

II

John Cage was stood in an echoless cell
hearing two sounds.

The highest was his central nervous system,
the lowest the circulation of his blood.

There is sound as long as you live
and there shall be sound after you die.

For music, Cage wrote in Silence,
There is, after all then, still hope.

trans. P.C. Evans

Learn Your Words

Boys, if you are unhappy,
once said our teacher of Greek,

then you must learn your words, learn
your words. He nodded with energy

so that ash fell on his vest,
but that was already filthy.

We laughed, half moved,
half with compassion, for the tragedy

was we knew it all, and he,
very old, almost fifty, nothing practically.

And that it would depart if only
you learned your words, that was something

so absurd, so completely silly
that it began to circulate as

a sort of wingèd word. It flutters
about me sadly now

for I would learn the words later
with which you can dispel the monster

and because I can no longer say
how I sometimes long for that voice,
for that ham-fisted advice.

trans. P.C. Evans

Garden, Dordrecht Museum

When I am dead
in the garden of this museum
above the bustle of the rushing leaves
a blackbird will just as clearly sing
on just so late a day in spring.

And I, I shall be there no longer
to forget with this singing
that in the course of time I have to die.

But on the other hand
– you never know –
I might outlive that bird.
And if I lie yet beneath the sods,
then my son shall hear
a blackbird sing so clear
on just so late a day in spring.
And he shall know who I was,
And ah, a bird knows nothing.

Though on the other hand again:
if blackbirds could think about their fathers,
then maybe they'd croak like a raven.

trans. P.C. Evans

From Black Sonnets

With difficulty I still know
How terribly I could hate you.
If I heard your knuckles crack as it drew
To that too punctual hour for you to go
To bed; and how I fought so
With myself not to fall asleep, knew
That everything you could not leave alone,
Was everything for which I had no use:

Your strict code, your stern belief.
And though I bowed my head when we
Sat at table to eat our bacon,
For I did not want to hurt you.
I could no longer speak to you then.
I, the stranger, who loved you.

trans. P.C. Evans

Empty Church

I

The tall carcass, the useless space,
organ and pulpit covered, an emptiness
that sucks the light inside it.

The boy who sat there on the rock-hard,
now-removed pews, imagined once
how, like Tarzan, you could swing

from chandelier to chandelier, and evade
the gentle compulsions
that stiffened the flock beneath him.

What remained is an absence
filling the whole space and stretching
to the barrel-vaulting, to the cranium

of one who stands intact here
and shall shortly leave this sanctuary behind.

II

The tombstones, on the other hand,
have just been laid outside, stacked
like the bodies they once covered.

The tombstones themselves were only laid bare
when the planks of the floor were taken away.
Yet, they are terribly worn

at least what there was of relief: the arms,
the festoons, the chubby cheeks
of cherubs, their once playful genitals

eroded to a semi-colon; only
what was inscribed can still be read
but is no longer of any importance.

trans. P.C. Evans

Song

There in the farthest wing
Beyond the expansive greens
The sisters are turning in pairs
Around and around the sheets

The sheets are rising and falling
With a regular rate
The sisters indeed should be singing
As well as they operate

Then the very last of the sheets
With a firm hand is unfurled
And into the air the last Jonah
Jubilantly is hurled

I turn myself around and you're there
Still in the cage of your bed
Greedily sucking the moisture
From the wads in water dipped.

Soon the white sisters will be coming
And they make almost no sound
The sheets will just have to wait
Till the whale first spits you out

trans. P.C. Evans

All The Tears

Que deviennent toutes les larmes
qu'on ne verse pas?
              Jules Renard

Two times I've seen my father sob,
the first time to my amazement
for I had just run away
from home, when I was four, but only
to see the rest of the world,
and not because it didn't suit me at home.

The second time was when he heard,
sitting in his armchair by the Erres-radio,
how the Dutch army
had capitulated to the Germans.
I had meanwhile grown so old
as to be severely embarrassed.

But much later, when I wanted to tell
how no more than two times
I'd seen my father cry, a half-way through
I could go no further, there was something in my
throat, something which wouldn't come out, something
stuck fast, something which almost choked me.

trans. P.C. Evans

Change Of Prospect

The view now brought back to this
end of a tiled roof,
a sky through the tangle
of a forgotten TV antenna.

The high window to be reached if needs be
by ladder, but why?
It sits fast as the wall
within which it's contained.

But it lets the light in from above
which could stream out of eternity
if one believed in that.

Sometimes it falls on a hand, a fist,
a wad therein which should like to moan
but came no further
than rustling.

And then again it strikes a head
which looks up and sees:
there is air-mail blue;

bringing him someone inside
who ground fine lavender
and once held her fingers
beneath his nose.

Never before
has there been such a modesty
of lust.

Who Writes History

You walked beside me
in your golden coat.
(21 November 1981)

Do you have that jacket still of gold,
that even then was peeled and worn?
Through the cracks you saw the moss-green leather.

How different it was to walk beside you
than when, between other soldiers,
I marched with a gun.

Other old servicemen
then wrote in the air:
Go demonstrate in Moscow.

Who writes history?
Not they who with their lightest steps
walk together in well-trod parade.

But also not those critical gentlemen
who from citadel or chamber
would think to dictate to a tidal wave.

An outing of the human sea. Or was it more?
A new beginning or fresh wine
for old poetry? I only know:

We walked together in happiness then, there,
in love with a hundred thousand people
and with each other.

trans. P.C. Evans

REMCO CAMPERT

Poetry is an Act...

Poetry is an act
of affirmation. I affirm
I live, I do not live alone.

Poetry is a future, thinking
of next week, of another country,
of you grown old.

Poetry is breath, moving
my feet, sometimes with hesitation,
over the demanding earth.

Voltaire had a pox, but
cured himself by drinking 200 pints
of lemonade amongst other things: and that's poetry.

Or take the surf. Beaten to bits
on the rocks but not beaten,
resumes the assault and thus is poetry.

Each written word
is an onslaught upon old age.
Death wins at last, for sure,

but death is merely the silence in the theatre
when the last word is spoken.
Death is an emotion.

trans. Graham Martin & John Scott

Sparrows

I,
no, it was Caligula, fat,
half-bald and 29
(you remember that winter),
died
a dishonourable, prosaic death
in the darkened entrance to a theatre
at the whispering hands of an assassin.

Caligula (jackboots, once
jovial, prodigal, human),
not in the claws of a beast,
but between the thighs of his sister
'which seemed to him an excellent Egyptian custom',
but no lustre
in the darkened entrance to a theatre.

But what am I talking about? About
the bygone gristle
of someone who, it turned out, was a sparrow,
thin skull, no god, no golden rain,
naked as men,
as sparrows, as sparrows
and men. Done to dust
at the shabby hands of the ludicrous world.

trans. Graham Martin & John Scott

Smashing Something

Today shall I for once smash something up?
A bit of culture for instance
but where can I so easily lay hands on that?
My marriage or the glasses of the panting
telegraph-boy:
'script in our hands at latest Friday'.
The bed
that's something I'd really enjoy kicking to hell
if I didn't have to sleep in it myself.
And what about the fat soft toy
and after that a hole in the sky.

How many have already been murdered in their sleep?
Far less by Christ
than those done in wide awake.

The cunning
of the directors of Union Miniëre
is something I'd rather be without –
at least not all the time.
Rather than that a mercenary,
from Indo-China through Algeria to the Congo,
fighting
in the pay of one or other body
and of his own.

Someone really ought to tell me
just precisely how a gun fits together.

trans. Graham Martin & John Scott

The Hague

Everywhere grimy roofs
green copper steeples
brackish air: corroded houses
moth-eaten meadow, neglected sea
O and the sad slow yellow trams
the gooseflesh of windblown streets
The Hague was a panorama Lent
every day a royal washed-out birthday

My grandfather unshaven
wandered like Strindberg through the house
trapped in his own dressing-gown

Playsick and embarrassed I was,
with my little rubber knife
disciplined bedlamite
I ambushed the standard-lamp
or the old purple cushion in the attic.

In a Moment of Depression

35 years, still not knowing the reasons
straying always further
in ever tougher shoes

did I really hear all this
once, when things were still to begin
when my socks slipped down, and snow was a feast day
when I sat by the stove reading
when I played football for the local lads
when the pinetrees smelt of sweet Caporal

– or did I invent it all

up on the wall now a photo of Humphrey Bogart
my wife and Jane Fonda
Truffaut and one of me –
the weather is in my mirror
my books smell of mildew
from all the houses where they've lain
and I'm getting a double chin

Listen carefully you that still write with a pencil
still paint with one finger
yell down alleys
and are sitting in the Odeon by half-past nine

listen carefully to what I omit.

trans. Graham Martin & John Scott

Mumbling

The clearer I want to say it
the worse the words I utter
it seems to me a phenomenon typical
of one thing and another

I'd really like to die, sometimes,
on some mornings
in November
when the letter-boxes are redder

on the other hand:
I'm still well provided for
provided with wife provided with daughters
provided with my mother
and comfortably
well-heeled in my shoes

O that'll be a sad sad day
the 1st day of the year 2000
70 I'll be then, an old man
someone for whom the 21st century arrived too late

Yes with my children's children on my knee
I'll be that day
1 sad old man

Had Rupert Brooke
not died so young
and was still alive
then he'd be 80 odd

But that's something you really
shouldn't think about too much

My poetry
say the boys who ought to know
is not so finely chased
as it used to be

Quite right too
for it's true of me
my finer corners are slowly rubbing off

trans. Graham Martin & John Scott

Poet

With the entire artillery
in one hand
under a black sky I stood,
a sky a-murmur with prayers.

On a blank wall the people pinned
the word:
Calamity,
leaving no single letter out.

My eyes they would believe no more.
My eyes they did forswear
and sent me home to a house,

to a house with rotting teeth,
a house surrounded by water,
but a chimney full of birds.

And a white wall to begin with
and later, perhaps, a boat
to go from house to house.

Sent me home they did,
with a bag full of sounds
in one hand,
the entire artillery
in the other.

trans. Graham Martin & John Scott

Churches

> Churches
still stand everywhere, they're
always being rebuilt.
Inside you can always find
one or two women, praying for nephews,
for their own salvation and so for the world's.

It's quiet in the churches, quieter
than the country on a windless day.
Cold, too, colder than
on a frozen lake. Quiet and cold
the churches are: serene, they say.
You can sing in them
at times appointed.

Churches stand in town and village
throughout this land, like
filling stations:
> a man in
overalls polishes the windows, fills
the tank, takes the money, goes
inside, reads his paper.

   trans. James Brockway

Avignon

In every inn
there was room for us. A bed
four walls, wallpaper crazy, a window
clay-coloured roofs, a courtyard with doves
a sky pink with rain: evening
in Avignon.

I read *Le Monde*.
Progressive capital lay tepid
in my wallet. I was complete and
myself entirely dirty with travel, longing for more dirt,
proof of progress. But one hand
held me back

For you sat
by me and in you died
a feeling, a move long before birth
your belly lay pale as lamplight under your clothes
and hidden beneath its skin reined in like horses
a death.

A tree is
fruitful and eternal, but
a person dies before he knows he lives,
blue for premature and noble, red for vain-spilt
blood, with a white bird between breast and shoulders
dead before breath
became earth.

Invisible

O in Ostend
it was so perfect
in the little hotel
in the rain

I was not available
that gentleman, said the *patron*
oh no, *connais pas*
no he's left already
it's a pity *madame*
c'est rien madame, tele-phoneys
to my love

whilst I stood
in the station foyer
hidden behind the latest news
leering at the English schoolgirls
with their little knapsacks,
assuming the protective
colour of the wall

or at nights
wrapped in my sand-coloured raincoat
flat out on the beach
waving at the lights
of the Dover boat

O sir
I thought you'd left already
we never see you these days, a shame
not even for breakfast
you must forgive us
madame will really be upset and
the season's been so bad

Invisible, I thought
I'm invisible
and in deadly joy became one
with the flowering toad in the vestibule
with the grey cobbles of the church square
with the cyclists on a washed-out holiday
with the seashell doll in the souvenir shop

and one with my love
who took certainty for uncertainty

and came

(for Deborah)

HUGO CLAUS

Elephant

I met that elephant,
Soaked to the skin in the rain. 'Hello, Jumbo.' 'Hello, Sir.'

We became friends, as one does.
I get on well with animals with trunks.
He found me, I think, a bit timid.
I on the other hand was entranced by his benevolence.
And by his majesty,
because isn't the elephant the emblem of the world,
four pillars supporting a globe of anthracite?

Often, at full moon, as one does,
he would waft coolness towards me
with a young birch in his trunk,
as if he were King of the Palms.

Then one day (why? I had done him no harm!)
I caught a look of his.
A look of ice, the look of a plaice,
without a glimmer of pity
in those round, tin eyes.

Then I donned my wishing cloak
put on my wig of pubic hair
and on top of that my dream cap
with circles, stars and stripes,
and then I recited a murderous formula
from the Catalogue of Shifting Signs.
The elephant died on the spot.
Without a sigh, he collapsed on his foundations,
and crumbled, turned to dust, went to ash,
and the ash in the grass shot upwards
in another shape, that of an oleander.

I cut it off at the roots.
Now it stands next to me on the terrace
shining and stinking. But
there is something I miss, I don't know what it is,
but I don't want to look any more.

Brother

'It's hard,' he said, 'bloody damned hard.
And unfair, the first time I've ever lost weight.'

Then the autumn outside, maize to the horizon,
the word slips out, horizon, orison.
Then not one word more from him.

In his gullet the plastic pipe.
He hiccups for hours. Can't swallow.

Still movement in the right hand
that carries the left like a fat lily.
The hand sticks its thumb up.
He goes on signing till his final decline.

He has soft white child's skin now.
He squeezes my anxious hand.

I search for a likeness, ours,
uneasiness from her,
impatience from him (no time for time),
the suspicion and naivety of both
and I'm back in our very first past,
that of a world like a meadow with frogs in
like a ditch full of eels
and later bets, table tennis,
domestic rules, the 52 cards,
the three dice
and always the unbridled hunger.
(I'm growing old instead of you.
I eat pheasant and smell the woods.)

His accommodation's made to size now.
The machine breathes for him.

Slime is suctioned away.
A rattle from his midriff,
and then his last movement, a languid wink.

Transmigration of souls. An ordering. A portion amputated.
The body still diminishing
and then suddenly in his face that was dead
a frown and a cramp
and then a wide-eyed, raging look,
unbearably clear, the fury and terror
of a tyrant. What does he see? Me, a man
who turns away, a coward surprised at his tears?
Then it is morning and they untie the straps.
And he for good

trans. Paul Vincent

Halloween

Our mirth the musicke of division.
Sir Walter Raleigh

I

It's quiet as the death of a dead man nobody knows
everywhere outside your room
where you dance by yourself as before.
But there too I hear
what you don't say.
Far from dishevelled Europe
over which the deadly haze is about to descend
we stand and stare at each other
almost dead like plastic chairs
and neither you nor I owning up to the murder of me or you.

II

On the black rubber floor
lies the autumn leaf, yellowed over the weekend.
Greedily you nibble a small block of ice
in the shape of a heart.
November comes, bringing inside the year's
bleaker end.
Time to pretend.
If I were a bog corpse, would you be my friend?
If I were gaga, laugh at me?
You nibble at me, not for real,
for that I'm too old and too cold.
Eros, a brat in cement,
arrives right on cue and crumbles to bits.

III

Mountains with coyotes and rattlesnakes,
in the valley the stinking cars
and in the bed with twelve pillows, you on your back.
You too grow more seedy, more toothless,
but not this afternoon.
Although you already mumble more colourlessly,
stumble more batlike out of bed.
You, once marble, once with hair sprayed green,
are more and more engrossed
in a story about yourself
even when you listen blindly to
hear if somewhere overseas the bleep
of your lover's wristwatch peeps.

IV

Ah, the happy hour, Bloody Mary's at half price,
they make you creative, inventive,
more, more, you become star material
(including the malignant growth
you cannot reach to scratch).

Fuck Halloween, All Hallows,
Return of the flocks, running riot of demons.
Who's at the door? Jesus, the dead are coming!
Come on in, sweeties. With which of the gentlemen
would you like to copulate?
With me? With little me?
With this rotten turnip, this shapeless material?

Scuse me dears, before you put out my candle
please degrade me and dazzle me still further.
Gas me, trick or treat, in an ultimate orgasm.

V

What do I know on the eve of the first of November?
That one must sow hemp at the midnight hour,
that last week you tasted of ginger,
that the great cold sets in on a day like tonight,
that you laugh at me like a cross-eyed nurse,
that the sun wrecks the lungs, that the moon wrecks the womb,
that's it's time to burn all the cardboard boxes
of the past before I forget,
that each of us feeds on another,
that you're like the mountains of Carmel,
gleaming and salt as the sea,
my crippled doe, my model with the runs,
my nun hungry for clothes and mirrors and
the coming of men who grunt,
and that you groan in your sleep without me.

VI

Your palate oily against my tongue
Then you slept and said, 'I wish I wanted to with you.'
Then at daybreak you watched TV
Where a barber won a trip to paradise.
Then coyotes and stockbrokers again roamed
your sleep,
haemoglobin dripped down your thighs.
Mene tekel, marmot.
I heard you dreaming.
The thanatologist that I am in my spare time
calculated that at most I'll
see a dozen more summers.
And when you woke up again, light as the day,
I assumed your camouflage,
itself a reason to go on living,
for the rest, suit yourself
about my mating game.

trans. Paul Vincent

Ostend

There my life started to decay.
Nineteen I was, I'd snore
In the Hôtel de Londres on the top floor.
The mail boat sailed under my window.
Each night the town threw itself away
On the waves.

Nineteen I was, played cards for fun
With the fishermen of the Iceland run.
They came from the Great Cold,
Their eyes and eyelashes full of salt, and
Bit into hunks of raw
Pork meat.
Ah, the clicking of dice. In those days
Of darts and dice I won always.

Then at dawn past the cathedral,
That stone tissue of fear,
Along the deserted dikes, the Kursaal.
The all-night bars
With the hollow-eyed croupiers,
The bankrupt bankers, English girls with TB.
And from the turquoise sea
The cruel screech of the seagulls.
'Come in, Mister Windy Wild,'
Yells an excited child
And over Ostend blows a cloud of sand
From the far shore's invisible strand
Hazy England
And the Sahara.

Past the shop fronts of chemists who back then
Sold condoms in a whisper,
Past the pier and the breakwaters,
The sea monsters in the fish den,
The race course where one Sunday
I stopped winning.

Sundays that came and went.
Nights in the Hotel of the Spas
Where I started at her oohs and aahs,
Her song, her lament.
Her sound still ravages my
Memories.
Other islands, deserts, mains
I have known, Istanbul that castle in the air,
Chieng-Mai with its landmines,
Zanzibar in the cinnamon glare,
The slow, slow Tagus. Their signs
Steadily disappear.

Sharper in the light of the North
I see the childlike face
Of the Master of Ostend tucked into his beard.
He was made of gristle,
Then of wax,
Now in bronze.
The bronze in which he
Smiles at his stone-dead youth.

trans. Paul Vincent

JUDITH HERZBERG

Target

A woman aged sixty-six
puts a thread through a needle,
that is – tries to. Now
the thread doesn't want to, bends,
splits in two, blurs.
Then there hardly seems to be
an eye in the needle (and if
there is an eye it is very
narrow, and askew).
The needle moves,
trembles, as if afraid
of the thread,
but the thread itself
is not convinced.
Above her someone
flies with a bomb.
A boy. Precision.

trans. Shirley Kaufman

The Way

The way you sometimes get to a room, not knowing why,
and then have to figure out what you were after,
the way you take something out of a closet
without feeling around for it and only after you hold it
know what you were looking for,
the way you bring a package somewhere
and when you leave are startled, feeling too light,
the way you wait for someone, fall madly in love
for a second with anyone passing, and still go on waiting.
The way you know I've been here once, what was it about,
until a smell comes back to tell you what,
the way you know whom to be careful with
and whom not, whom you can lie down with –
that's the way animals think, I think,
the way animals know the way.

trans. Shirley Kaufman

Sentimental

They are sitting in the car in a traffic jam,
the radio is on, exhaust fumes
and music, a song he thinks
is beautiful, about
violins on fire and a dance which goes on
until the end of love.
Not the song but what he says
makes her unable to look at him.
Now something else enters the car:
music and exhaust fumes and shyness.
Shyness because the dance
until the end of love is much too much
stretches too far into the past,
too far ahead, his soul
swells suddenly unprotected, so unprotected,
she only says: 'Sentimental'.
Yes he says, sentimental.
She will never know if he knew
how she seized upon that word.
He will never know what she
understood, how far and far,
she will never know that he
understood that she understood
what suddenly came over him, unless
someone, an historian perhaps,
later exactly reconstructs the way it used to go
with people in traffic jams with radios.

trans. Rina Vergano

Welcome in Free World

'I'll speak a basic English:
You cold, warm, hunger have?
You university – oh – yes.
Where? Where is that? No,
sorry, far away, for me.

You can be quiet now.
Your troubles over.
They don't come here
they don't come back
to get you. Here is
safe. No worry.

No, wailing sound
is of a sick car.
Siren of ambulance.
They go to hospital,
normal, in haste,
other cars must make space.

These clothes here
you can keep. They
look so good on you.
You don't believe?
Oh, not your taste.
You have? Sorry –
I thought that over there –
Well. Yes. No, they
are not new.

But for you they are!
New. Yes, and a mattress,
a whole own bed
sheets pillows
towel, soap. No?
Not lie down?
Why not lie down.
You cannot stay
standing. You can't.

You cannot stand
for nights on end just
like that next to bed.
As if waiting for –
someone. No one
said: dead. Just
we don't know. You
must not worry so.

Yes you can stay.
Stay long? How long?
I cannot say. Stay
means so many
different things anyway.'

Blue Anemones

Bunch of thirty blue anemones.
One has a few kinks in its stem,
at every kink a new angle.
The only flower that looks straight out.
Don't think this is the poet.
He doesn't know yet
which of the thirty is him.
Doesn't even know he's going to get
blue anemones.

trans. Shirley Kaufman

Between

Between your shoulder and your ear
I see the gray underside of a ping-pong table.
Leaning against it is a parasol with black
and dirty-white stripes and a whitish fringe.
A pale yellow bedspread lies folded
across a chair. This painting doesn't need
to be painted and can't be anyway.
It suggests what clouds do from an airplane window
suggests the true difference between ah! and gone.

trans. Shirley Kaufman

The Heart

For the heart it was a chance.
It throbbed with interest
strong-willed it waited
it still had so much punch.

The whole world watched, read,
saw photos of white coats,
thought of the man, how
he, perhaps, could carry on.

Everyone's dream. The heart
pumped as staunchly as it could
pumped as it always
did, always had done.

It was an exact match. Everything
was there and matched exactly.
But there was something that
did not take part, did not join

in welcoming the heart.
No-one knew what it was.
Everyone's fear: that it
would not take. It did not take.

Everyone thought of the man,
no-one thought of the heart,
how it, still so vital even
in these foreign ribs, got jammed.

And when it was buried, no-one hurried to the churchyard,
no-one shouted: 'Hey, wait, here a heart is being
buried in a breast which has rejected it. If it must be committed to
the mud at least put it with its own flesh and blood
for even if that's long since decayed,
here it has no chance of rest and certainly not eternal, more like
eternal brooding that perhaps,
despite the thumping and the pumping
it was his fault. I'll pay the transport!'

trans. Rina Vergano

Song

It always takes much longer than you think,
even if you think
it's bound to take much longer than I think
it still takes longer
than you think.

It is always more expensive than you think,
even if you think
it's bound to be more expensive than I think
it's even more expensive
than you think.

It is more trouble than you think
even if you think
it's bound to be more trouble than I think
it's much more trouble
than you think

It goes more quickly than you think
even if you think
it's bound to go much quicker than I think
it's still
quicker than you think.

Boxes

Because all through the war we always heard
about before the war and how naive
they were, I am very careful now.
If I throw out something, for instance
a carton, I hope
that box will never catch up
with me in the shape of blame:
just think how innocent,
to throw out boxes,
if only we'd kept one,
kept only one!

trans. Shirley Kaufman

The Waiting at the Bus-Stop

The seeing of a taxi.
The thinking: not yet. I've only just got here.
The noticing someone else arrive.
The sizing up of him/her.
The pretending I'm not looking at him/her.
The not pretending I'm not looking at him/her.
The looking past him/her into the distance as if to see if bus is
        coming.
The really looking into the distance.
The thinking: is that the bus?
The continuing to look until it comes closer.
The seeing that it is not a bus, but a large truck.
The thinking: shall I take a taxi after all?
The thinking: I might as well have taken the first taxi. I've waited
all this time for nothing if I take a taxi now.
The noticing two other people arrive at the bus-stop.
The seeing that these two are not yet impatient.
The thinking: they're thinking it will be here soon.
The guessing what these two do together.
The sizing up of them unobtrusively.
The feeling surprised at the first waiting person, who doesn't look
        at the new two at all. Is not curious. Is only waiting.
The thinking: what if we take a taxi with the four of us.
The wondering where the others are going.
The getting cold.
The seeing of many buses going in the opposite direction.
The thinking: where are they all, they must come back this way
        eventually.
The imagining of the terminus, the turning.
The thinking: if I take a taxi it's expensive and I've wasted all that
        time now anyway.
The remembering of the same thought from yesterday.
The remembering remembering the same thought yesterday.

The deciding: I'm just going to take a taxi.
The waiting for a taxi.
The seeing full taxis passing by.
The thinking: tomorrow I'll take the first empty taxi straight away.
The remembering of the same thought from yesterday.
The thinking that it can't be much longer now before the bus comes.
The imagining of an enormous traffic jam in the distance.
The contemplating walking.
The imagining how the bus will drive past before I have reached the
        next stop.
The thinking that walking warms one up.
The forbidding oneself to look to see if bus is coming.
The counting of cars.
The forbidding oneself to look to see if bus is coming until at least a
        hundred cars have gone past.
The seeing of many empty taxis among the cars.
The thinking that it makes no sense to take a taxi now.
The thinking that now it is actually high time to take a taxi.
The considering to write this down one day.
The wondering if other people also think like this.
The wondering what the objective right moment is to take a taxi:
        immediately, after waiting a short time or after waiting a
        long time.
The remembering of parents who never took a taxi.
The trying to remember special occasions when parents did take a
        taxi.
The noticing how crowded it has become at the bus-stop.
The thinking: at a full bus-stop – wait, at an empty bus-stop – take
        a taxi.
The realising how much it would cost
to take a taxi every day.
The calculating that this would be less expensive
than owning a car.
The imagining how it would be to have a flat tyre
on a deserted autostrada in howling wind and pouring rain.
The realising that the cars are driving past without being counted.

The realising that after thirty or forty the mind has wandered.
The estimating that it was more like two hundred.
The seeing on the watch that only six minutes have passed.
The being thankful that it is not raining.
The drinking of a cup of tea in the imagination.
The wondering if there are any biscuits in the house.
The fright at realising that the key –
The discovering of the key in the other pocket.
The imagining how far six minutes walking –
The deciding that it stinks.
The thinking of the many murders of taxi drivers.
The imagining of a blood-smeared empty taxi.
The wondering if other people also think of murder so often.
The wondering if murderers think of murder often.
The thinking not.
The not knowing why not.
The wondering if other people also often wonder
what other people are wondering.
The wondering if other people ever wonder
what I wonder.
The not noticing that the bus has come.

RUTGER KOPLAND

Natzweiler

1

And there, beyond the barbed wire, the view –
very charming landscape, as peaceful
as then.

They would need for nothing, they would
be laid down in those green pastures,
be led to those peaceful waters,

there in the distance. They would.

2

I trace the windows of the barrack huts,
watch-towers, gas-chamber.

Only the black reflection of distance
in the panes, of a peaceful landscape,

and beyond it, no-one.

3

The dead are so violently absent, as though
not only I, but they too
were standing here,

and the landscape were folding their invisible
arms around my shoulders.

We need for nothing, they are saying,
we have forgotten this world.

But these are no arms,
it is landscape.

4

The yellowed photos in the display cases,
their faces ravaged by their skulls,
their black eyes,

what do they see, what do they see?
I look at them, but for what?

Their faces have come to belong
to the world, to the world
which remains silent.

5

So this is it, desertion, here is
the place where they took their leave,
far away in the mountains.

The camp has just been repainted, in that gentle
grey-green, that gentle colour
of war,

It is as new, as though nothing
has happened, as though
it has yet to be.

trans. James Brockway

The Fairground

Dear grandfather, who art in heaven
in that white light of August, high

above the fairground, this I was,
this child, here, in the depths, look down on him,

look how death has taken nothing away,
has preserved everything, left it as it was,

has laid it still: the goat with the eyes,
the sleeping donkey, the monkey in the wirework,

laid still: the blood-red roundabout, the lion
with the rusty saddle, the screeching see-saw,

laid still: the shouting and crying, the smells
of iron and oil, the dirty clouds of dust,

laid still, the thumping heart in the maze,
the mirrors with giants and dwarves a-giggle,

laid still: that surge of desire in his back,
and when it was over, that throat full of grief,

laid still, dear grandfather, up there in heaven,
look: this child, here in the depths.

trans. James Brockway

Still Life with Golden Plover

Things are lying there on the table, but

why – it is winter and they're lying there
again, a few old apples, grey parsley,
a shrivelled onion, a golden plover, dead,

They're asleep in a frozen world, in
an orchard, a kitchen garden, a ditch,
they're dreaming they have been found, taken home,

laid down on that table – but why,

for there is no-one who knows how vast
the winter is, how unending its pity,
how reverently it chooses what may die.

I've forgotten what I see, I must have
laid them down, and not
come back, left them there like that.

trans. James Brockway

Thanks to the Things

1

The morning when the things again come back
to life, when low light shines out of
the mahogany, table silver, porcelain,

the bread again begins to smell of bread,
the flowered teapot of tea,
the air of old people,

when, in the dead-still room, there comes
a muttering, Lord, bless this day too,
to all eternity, amen.

2

The afternoon when things again become
the afternoon, light flecks like butterflies
begin to dance in white and waving curtains,

the fruit bowl again begins to smell of fruit,
the chairs of cane, the bouquet in the vase
of lilacs, the flower-pot of earth,

when, in the dead-still verandah, knitting needles
begin to click, the newspaper to rustle again,
the gate squeaks, the gravel softly crunches.

3

The evening when the things again begin to long
to disappear, the red carpet, the brown
velvet curtains yearn for the darkness,

the pipe in the ash-tray smells again of smoke,
the banana of its fruity flesh, the milk
of the steaming milk of bedtime,

when, in the dead-still room, the Word
is heard again, the Book claps to,
silence falls again, the pendulum clock ticks.

4
The night when the things again begin to be
but shadows of themselves,

the room again begins to smell of laundered sheets,
old woodwork, lavender,

when the dead-still window breathes again
with sleeping treetops in the wind.

5
The moment when, call it
a morning, an afternoon,
an evening, a night,

when the things begin again,
call it a house where light,
scents and sounds come
and go,

but it is death that is searching
for words for the moment when
I, and whatever he may say,
I am that.

Message of the Isle of Chaos

How long we have been here now, friends,
it was once meant to be a holiday
but what it is now –

We saw the folder: Chaos, ladies and gentlemen,
Your island: the glossy photographs,
the bright blue bay of Chaos,
the chalk-white fishing village of Krisis.

We read that the island is praised for
its deep, deep quiet,
the last inhabitants are even
called happy under their plane tree.

We thought it was a joke
and went there, but whether it was so –
we sit on the quay
every day

And at our feet lies one of the dogs
every day, afraid we might be leaving.

We can see the Hagia Katastrophi
lying there at anchor, everything
being slowly shit white by the gulls,
lying there waiting for passengers.

How long by now, our story grows still
stranger the longer it lasts.

Should this message ever reach you
or should it not.

trans. James Brockway

Johnson Brothers Ltd

In those days when my father was still big,
dangerous tools in the bulging pockets
of his jacket, in his suits the odours
of teased out twine and lead,
behind his eyes the incomprehensible world
of a man, gas-fitter, first-class,
said mother, in those days how different
my feelings were, when he would shut the doors
on her and me.

Now he is dead and I am suddenly as old as he,
it turns out to my surprise that he too had
decay built into him. In his diary I see
appointments with persons unknown, on his wall
calendars with gas-pipe labyrinths,
on the mantlepiece the portrait of a woman
in Paris, his woman, the incomprehensible
world of a man.

Looking into the little hand-basin of porcelain
dating from the thirties, with its silly pair of lions,
Johnson Brothers Ltd., high up in the dead-still
house the shuffle of mother's slippers,
Jesus Christ, father, here come the tears
for now and for then – they flow together
into the lead of the swan-neck pipe,
no longer separable from the drops that come
from the little copper tap marked 'cold'.

trans. James Brockway

Breughel's Winter

Winter by Breughel, the hill with hunters
and dogs, at their feet the valley with the village.
Almost home, but their dead-tired attitudes, their steps
in the snow – a return, but almost as

slow as arrest. At their feet the depths
grow and grow, become wider and further,
until the landscape vanishes into a landscape
that must be there, is there, but only

as a longing is there.

Ahead of them a jet-black bird dives down. Is it mockery
of this laboured attempt to return to the life
down there: the children skating on the pond,
the farms with women waiting and cattle?

An arrow underway, and it laughs at its target.

trans. James Brockway

When, Where?

It's autumn and the dogs are at it again.
There's no tenderness among dogs.

Say something, she says. Only a child can know
what I feel. I'm a child no more.

Tenderness, that's, I say, as I take
her breasts firmly in my hands,

that's the answer to a question that's
not been asked. The odour of every autumn,

I mean, the question when, where
was it and the answer to that.

I can smell your hair again, we're sitting
against each other on a bench in the gardens.

I feel what a child feels when it sees
what we are doing. What we are saying is nonsense.

Father, I See your Face

Father, I see your face again, years
after your death – almost a shadow
in this vastness, a shadow
white with heat – lonely
stone in the sky, the sea.

Head of a Roman general, nose
flattened, mouth torn open,
eye-sockets vacant, raised to
the sun, in a desert.

Almost a scream still at
this death.

Father, your face there, a sort of
island where no-one
has ever lived, where
no-one ever arrives.

trans. James Brockway

Autistic

Fine little body, dear miniature machine,
it is a child, I think,

I look and it looks like eyes of glass,
like windows, outside and inside, together,
like this at everything there is,

I speak and it listens like an ear to a shell,
to that rustling void, that sound
so far and so near, together, so everywhere,

I pick it up and it feels like too heavy a doll,
like a stone so much does it wish
to return to earth,

I bath it and it glides out of my hand
like the skin of a fish
into the water,

I listen and it makes a sound as though the voice
of a child was blowing in the wind,
lost and forgotten,

I think and whatever I think
it is still no child of mine.

I Cavalli di Leonardo

All those sketches he left behind –

endless series of repetitions: bunches of muscle, sinews,
knuckles, joints, the entire machinery
of driving-belts and levers with which
a horse moves,

and out of thousands of hair-thin little lines, the skin
almost invisibly gently disappearing into the paper
of ears and eyelids, nostrils,
skin of the soul –

he must have wanted to find out how a horse
is made and have realised
it can't be done,

how the secret of a horse grew and grew
beneath his pencil.

Made the most splendid designs, studied them,
discarded them.

trans. James Brockway

Michelangelo's David

Statues were not made, they had to be
'freed from the marble', as though they were
there already, always,

(somewhere, in a windless June, on a white
uninhabited island in a blue-green sea)

and he did indeed find a splendid stone,
under its skin a perfect machine
of brains, muscles and heart,

and no trace of effort, none of a movement
there had once been or still could be, simply
attitude, indifferent strength

of milliards of crystals, perfect
copy of a youth.

Michelangelo's Cristo Deposto di Croce

Old, 'so close to death, and so far from God',
he must have stood before this block of marble,

from which the splendid, youthful body of Christ
had already been released, though it hung limp

and dead in its mother's lap, and about
them an old man's arms, his face drained

of everything but grief, impotent ending,

his self-portrait. He had written: 'there is no
painting, no image now which sets the soul at rest,

the soul in search of divine love,
which opened its arms to us on the cross.'

He had wanted to be buried at the foot
of this statue, but smashed it and left

what remained of it ravaged, incomplete.

trans. James Brockway

WILLEM VAN TOORN

Translation

Again the fields are strange with frost.
The vivid odours of September, October.
He arranges the last things he saw
between the farmyard and the horizon:
a jinking hare, the printed dew;
the patch of bald earth

where nothing ever grew;
the hunter's track deep into the polder,
studied for almost a hundred years;
the orchard's secret baby owls.
The earth he ploughed with horses
all his life. He knows it like his skin.
He laughs as the morning opens in his mind.

He is lost, lost in the housing estate,
lost for words to tell his horses
he is powerless to pass
beyond these buildings
that thwart him like a dream.
He wants a piss, shielded
by the willow. Which knows him.
Which has disappeared.

The kind young women who live here now
find him in their gardens.
They take him home, his old eyes
troubled like a two-year-old.
He was standing near the hedge.
The emptiness falls
through his head like manna.

Again he hears the childhood promise:
'I will take you back. Back to *melk en honing.*'

trans. Craig Raine

Fallow Land

The view is clean as cartridge paper
freshly pinned to a drawing board.
But marks long to emerge
and the eye searches for something.
Under the sand, you sense
the divine dirt of a pencil point.

The artist's fingers are just out of frame.
Only water, water and sand,
and a frisson of grass at the fringe.
Creation, containing creation –
upheaval's hosanna to the only human.

In the distance, dim ideas,
patiently waiting
for vision to make them visible.

trans. Craig Raine

House

You knew exactly where you were:
white string stretched along the foundations.
Eye contact with the spirit level
told you the walls were true.
Work table. Bed. Clean sheets.

But the blueprint blurs
in its portfolio. Under the floors,
grass writhes like albino wiring.
Take a look over your shoulder,

back there at the beginning,
and watch what was once so solid
give up the ghost. Walls so thin
the world shines through.

Your house existed before it was built.
All its detail was a dream.
Without love can perfection endure?

The idea is always eternal.
But not what we make of it.
Worn treads. Cramped corridors. A glory hole.
The gentle tick of time abrades even brick,
will wear away stone. Bet on it.

trans. Craig Raine

Sonsbeek, Stereo Photography

Layer after layer of vitrified time,
misted dim with distance so that I'm
surmising more than I see: your foot must be there,
hiding behind the plants by the path, your hair
blending with golden threads of autumn. But where
's the angle from which this can be read for sure?

In photos still tantalisingly unclear:
On the Bridge of Swans. The Belvedere.
Assembled places, from Lorentz to the Great
Falls. But all the images retreat
in double illegibility. Here, between
all this sepia, there's no life to be seen.

Maybe I need to change the way I gaze.
If I stare without expectation, it clicks into place.
Depth. Pin-sharp – the fathomless park.
Feet chastely together, you stand beside
the Pavilion. Six silver buttons shine
on your winter coat. A serious little face
beneath your fur hat. Your hands at your back.

Excursion, almost eighty years before.
I see the child who in her already bore
what she couldn't imagine: the big girl
the young woman, the bride, the mother, all
she would be. So enlarged it takes my breath
away, I see the smile coming which you'll
not have again till seconds before your death.

Landscape with Father

Sprawled flat on your back
you've become the hills, the banks
of scrub and stubbly brown
here, the wind-smoothed cracks

in your forehead of greyish stone.
On your cheek an ochre village.
In your palm an olive grove
grows over your fingers.

Now the season is hot
above your feet. The fleecy
clouds will soon be cooling
the evening. Sleepily cooing
doves make their cot
in the eaves of your hair.

When the rains come this winter, your eye
slowly opens: a clear
pool in summer's dry
bowl. Children lean
over your lids and peer
playfully inside.

What an amazed landscape. Not
even you, I bet, could have thought
that you would be so quiet.

★ ★ ★

I was trying to find you like this, it's true.
And also a nameless nothing
had almost taken the form of something
inside me that wasn't you,

at least not really, and but still
would have the sounds of your name
if it had speech. How

could I have dreamed that now,
before the window, you
would take precisely the shape
which fits in with the slip

you're putting on, with the light
whose rays infallibly strike
every hair framing your face
which exists in me just the same.

Irrgarten

'If here, o courtier, guest, you wish to escape
from death, think a little before you begin
of Theseus the Greek: don't walk recklessly in,
don't take just any path when you enter this maze.

Arm yourself with good thread, tied
fast beside the entrance, unwind it and find
your way back from the core, love's island.'

So what was there? Fallen leaves. A lion-
footed bench, black with damp. All trace
of your light girlish laughter long effaced.

The way back. Echoes. At every crossing
you tantalisingly slip away from me:
a foot, fold of your skirt over your knee,
swirl of your hair, irrevocably fled.

They do it with mirrors. How come this web of threads
here? And was this my path? Irrgarten: maze,
crazy garden. Who seeks you here must be mad.

trans. Francis R. Jones

Glumdalclitch

To her I chiefly owe my Preservation in that Country: We never parted while
I was there; I called her my *Glumdalclitch*, or little Nurse

Jonathan Swift, *Gulliver's Travels*, 'A Voyage to Brobdingnag'.

How did you get to be so big? You held me high
on your lap as we moved through the landscape. Grass
stood like a spiked wood, waving beside our path.
Of trees I only saw the start: the sky

where they stopped so far above
that leaves and birdflight had to be believed,
not seen. I was too small to stare
beyond your eyes, your windblown hair.

I dream it here again. On horseback. We ride
together for ever, through your thunderous land.
Sometimes you take me tenderly in your hand:
towering hamlets slide by its side.

You're resting in the grass. No end
in sight. The dream breaks where I'm about to blend
into you. Hills. The garden. Too big to comprehend.

Lilliput

The Treasurer took a Fancy to be jealous of his Wife, from the Malice of
some evil Tongues, who informed him that her Grace had taken a violent
Affection for my Person; and the Court-Scandal ran for some Time that she
had come privately to my Lodging.

      Jonathan Swift, *Gulliver's Travels*, 'A Voyage to Lilliput'

Now that you have reached this pass, tinier
than my little finger, me roaming
gigantic through my exile – though seas divide
us, with a single step I'm back inside

the memory of how you came. Gloaming.
Desire hovered like the half-light around
us. I was lying on the ground.
Your feet tickled past my mouth. You knelt
before my eyes. Reflection through which you went

life-size inside me. You drove up by the dwarfwood: I held
your coach in my hand, horses and all. Before
you climbed back in, you looked round once more.
Sadness came black with the night. I took refuge
in teeming darkness, fleeing your sleeping land.

Magnifying glass the poem. But nothing moves.
Empty unland in the hollow of my hand.

         trans. Francis R. Jones

December

Where the plan was made
that predicted how
this half-light, horizontal and grey,
would reach just in time
the waiting roofs it's touching now

above the city that precisely fits
into this year: the sluttish,
jaded but still sublime
bend of the *gracht*, the sooty
pride of gilded facades. What of all this

still filters into the slow-
ly tilting head of the man below
you in the street
with his cap of matted hair,
three coats, a supermarket trolley full
of plastic, as he stands for an age
beyond endurance on one leg, like a gull,
in the first hesitant snow.

How, according to plan,
this too is already past, now that your hand
is turning the last calendar page.

Hans Memling: Portrait of a Young Woman, Possibly Maria Moreel, 1480 (Later Named 'The Persian Sibyl')

Maybe Maria Moreel. We see her, at least.
She's held safe in her frame, too chaste
for words. So pale and *burgerlijk*, so
aloof and distantly well-to-do

that someone later went and gave her
the name of Sibyl. Wished it on her, rather –
thought her to Persia, so mythically far
that we can't reach her any more.

But she just wants to be here. Her hand – see
how it lies over the frame, as if she's been
waiting beside a stiff window that opens
suddenly, centuries later, into this moment.

trans. Francis R. Jones

The Poem

So you may never pass from sight
inside the poem I hold you tight –
the way you walk, the way you lie,
the way your body speaks to me.

In centuries still to be
a face alive and reading might
be bending, the better to see,
over the poem, the words I write
to put you down in black and white.

trans. Francis R. Jones

In Memoriam

I dreamt that you were lying beside me last night.
You were already sick. You said: I am
of death to the bone. Do you mind you can't come
in me? Just hold me gently close beside

you. I said: when I saw you, you were so white
and tired – and then invisible, hidden from sight
in a coffin where I walked down the path,
into the rain and the village. Waiting grass

lay next to the hole, the turfs stacked in a pile.
How come you're here again? You told me why:
I wanted to do what I'd left undone, to lie
beside you in bed and talk together as life.
But what I am now speaks no language we share.

The light wasn't on. So how could I see you there?
I fell asleep in my dream. While you were hold-
ing me tight. Late in the day, the room was still cold.

trans. Francis R. Jones

H.H. TER BALKT

She Carries a Glass of Water...

While rainbows throng at the window
oceans underfoot
she carries a glass of water up the stairs.

In her glass a bunch of poppies, fields
of golden grain and fireweed stars,
dust of evening villages like snow

flaking in the glass she's carrying up the stairs.
It's the big stairs from silence
to silence, the stairs there's an end to.

Demons, winter revellers –
away from the edge of her glass!
Bravely she carries her big glass of water.

Hear: in her Bermuda Triangle
boats and even faster planes are eager
to plunge and run aground, lips

eager to stick to her glass, ghosts,
drinking and crying 'There is the Sea, the Sea –'
(Four highways peep through the keyhole.)

She's carrying her glass of water up the stairs.
It's water like clear light shining,
roads in summer, cities, mountain peaks...

Held in the beams of the house she's in
on sailing ships of old the raging water
sings of love; and she is love.

The stairs were made of rumour and broke almost,
brittle as twigs of thought, but gracefully
she carries her glass of water.

(All stairs pine for the louder blaze,
houses pine for the eddy where all's
an end to ships and planes as well.)

But she carries her glass of clear water,
carries her glass up good-hearted stairs
and under her foot deep oceans purl.

trans. Lloyd Haft

China, June

The poet's but an elder bush
and blind. Murmuring he sings in wind
that climbs in him.

In June a poppy and a gentian
(secret silent lovers) bloomed above the Square.
Sullen roots of devilish quick grass... Flower trumpets
lured a thousand pluckers into light.

Raging loomed the chariots: threshers
of stone with rattling wheels of stone; loud
shrieked the whips in the hands of stone
that mowed away the poppy and the gentian.

The poet's but an elder bush
and blind. Silently he sinks in wind
that writhes upon him.

– June 15, 1989

trans. Lloyd Haft

Slim Waist

She's my elixir.
It's her slim waist.
Dangerous words
keep out of her way.

When she's not with me
her eyes and her waist
lighter than thistledown
linger over the meadows.

Trismegistus the alchemist
wrote on an emerald:
what's above is also
below. She's everywhere.

It's her slim waist
powers me.
Dust blows in from the cities
but it doesn't faze her.

What would a cloud be
without the look in her eyes.
What would the day be;
the thistle; the stone.

Ice massed; the thorn apple
raised its shadow.
Dangerous words
keep out of her way.

trans. Lloyd Haft

With Beef and an Oil Lamp

With beef and a lamp of porcelain
my mother lost her way down Poleman Road,
over the stoops and tiles bending low
with comforting crystals clinging to her hand.

Ships sail on a lamp of porcelain,
they lead the way with slanting sails.
The lamp was cradled in frozen beef
and gently on its way in the autumn dark.

The world bears us, bears us all the way.
Nothing it could ever do but bear us.
And out of the ironmonger's, saws and axes
glare at a shadow dragging by.

Cracking gently as leather in trains
or the ear in an airplane climbing,
needles of ice, needles of ice that gather
along the blackening roofs of Poleman Road.

They told you 'Get off in Z,
get off the train in Zutphen, off in Zutphen.'
You skated once, so swift your hair
was fragrant over the ponds, over the ponds.

With gifts in the train; in September.
It was a train that rode all through September.
Snow and sheet ice all along that train,
polar snow and sheet ice on that train.

The world bears us, bears us all the way.
Carries the cities, trains going back.
No saw, no axe awaits you on the platform.
Only your shadow, shadow.

With beef and a lamp of porcelain
my mother lost her way down Poleman Road,
past the dance hall and the ironmonger's,
slanting sails, bound for a bright land.

The needles of ice melted, turned to drips.
An oil lamp twinkles like a ship at sea,
golden clouds cover the golden moon.
Nobody saves the mind if once it strays.

And down on the street a bag of beef
and an oil lamp bright with boats,
off to a new, a high, a low, a land
that's bound to be, and not for you alone.

The Thaw Wind

Resin drips from the house of gall
in the thaw wind.
Resin drips from the heart, that pine
with its apple falling, red it falls
in the thaw wind.
Like a candle the ice melts
in the thaw wind.

The sixteenth-century march of the city,
pacing the city, pacing:
stone the cock of a thousand crests.
Red and green the cock revolves
above the city,
keeps to the course of the wind.

trans. Lloyd Haft

Owl

A fluffy little kitchen crock
among the two-edged needles: pines.
Grey under his hood, in the crown;
cheerlessly he drinks the mouse's tail;
a touch of night breeze makes him no gentler,
nor the whistle of the jet fighter,
nor the warden with his brisk pace,
greener than the pines.

Cheerlessly he spits his wad; sees
the carnival of the forests, ermine
the scurrying weasel, fluttering brood;
peaceful devastation, sweet slumber
of the pond. He seems calculating.
He loathes the jukebox of the songbirds.
Age-old wisdom: that's on his side.
Sagas drift through his head like leaves.

Diogenes in his tub: two lanterns
that shine out wider than candle flames
in his head with its ruffling down.
He touches up his claw, stretches.
Swiftly his wordless wings brush
edges of branches, tips of trees.
And back he flies to the bells
(home in darkness) that he hates.

trans. Lloyd Haft

Pig Elegy

There's something so sad in the wise eyes of pigs,
they look like prophets of a slaughter season.
(I'm not fond of prophets, and yourself? No,
more of a climbing evergreen.)
Their tusks torn out on the assembly line
as out they trek from mother, the body, exodus from hot Egypt,
through the Red Sea delivered and on to straw and the many-
bladed graven images of man.
Once in a while one, an old bear under the old
tree of knowledge (dying variety of apples)
standing still as death looks at wind on the horizon,
by insight blinder than by nature nearly.

You nearly see, in the bride-like autumn veils
in the tang of the whispering wind, the cloud
of thoughts turned on its top-heavy head: Striped I ran, boar
once, and what am I now! A pity for the tamed
pigs, of animals they are the poets,
melancholic and good for nothing much
till singed and on the wall their blubber
snaps like an elegy open.

trans. Lloyd Haft

ANNA ENQUIST

Nobody

Death, they say, hath taken.
But I was sitting on the ground with a dead man,
nobody came taking.

I said some words in baby talk that stayed unheard
as the last breath took off for the city and
nobody came taking.

The game had no object and in the end
even I knew it. Nobody

smashed us with a big fist
on the lousy pavement, just nobody.

trans. Lloyd Haft

Daughter, Daughter (1)

There aren't really elastic bands
fastening her to you,
you don't really jump when
fifteen miles down the road she
falls off her bike. You're inside
the petrified house, you
don't feel a thing.

She rides along the gleaming
tram tracks. My genes
whisper commands
in her body. She sings, shakes
her wet hair. Mom all over again,
she laughs. No, the boy's saying:
you, you, you.

Daughter, Daughter (2)

I'd rather be a hooded crow,
at the least whiff of wrong,
of ruckus: on wings,
no matter where to.

Or a windmill. Wouldn't I
show them, on National
Windmill Day.

Best of all: a river that could move
around it, move through it all.
The worst rage beat out
in the waterfall, now slow
and crafty.

I took the heated children
along, held onto them, gave them food
and carried them as far as the ocean.
Once we were there
we forgot it all.

Daughter, Daughter (3)

I *am* home now, you're saying,
have been for two days. I don't call that
home, it's a tight overnighter.
On the bed I sit
beside you, that's true, today
and tomorrow too. In the furnace room
I come across baby shoes, the light
blue ones; just can't help
crying even though downstairs you still
are, still go by your name in what we call
your own bed, you're saying two days.

Daughter, Daughter (4)

How can I explain. A kid
can't help it: weighs 130
now, lives in the city.

Mom manages the memories. The kid
remembers scrapbooks and a couple of songs.
No other break-up's so cruel. Always

knew (later, big) and never realized
time really was going to tear
the heart out, frayed edges and a

red hole would remain. You've got to
cover that over. They don't believe you. The kid
can't help it. It has pain too.

In the Woods

Blueberries blush their welcome
with swollen stems. Beeches
wait with their lightest green.

The oak leaf's about to fall,
it whispers, rustles under
your stumbling foot, murmurs farewell

around your walking stick. Blood refuses
to feed fingers and feet,
mottled glass grows on your eyes.

It smelled like the world here,
now it tastes bitter in your aged
mouth. Sun rips the woods open,

light points to the ground.
That's where you're going down, and the woods
stand whispering, waving above.

trans. Lloyd Haft

"I am poured out like water"

Stupid water. Beats and lashes the
piles of the bridge mutely bracing
itself against surrender. Century
on century, tying two shores is
what he knows. Tired, alert.

Again I go through the old city, always
to the river. Amidships I station myself
in powerless absorption, bare hand
on stone. I roar with cut throat,
without sound, with rage and loss:

All that we know, what we are like,
disappears like wind over the fields.
Memory thrashes in the water and is
lost. Grey-brown waves are not their
names. The mass murderer Time.

River, flow backwards. Stone,
be fire again. Air around me,
be body that carries me and
comforts. Memory, come undone.

trans. Lloyd Haft

Invasion

On the bare decline, wind in my hair,
we stand and you look. With all your might
you look at me, image of love.

And I, I crawl in through your
tear-filled eyes, slide down nerve paths,
hop over myelin sheaths; synapses
rustle, RNA forces proteins
to line up in my image:

I am carved, chiselled in your brain
till you die, until you die.

trans. Lloyd Haft

Poem

Wooden almost, the way he waits
in the distance for my footstep, his
starting gun. Way up on the dyke.

Down flat he goes, traces lightning
over the field, slams himself
home safe to his whirlpool of grass.

I don't want to hunt you, hare; I want
to share your wide-open house, I want
to read what you wrote in the field.

I want to feel your golden-grey fleece
but ever between the hand and the hare
the lie and the ruin crowd in.

A New Year

1

Not yet. The son still has to marry
and the old man die. There's still going to be
World Cup soccer and a spawn of goldfish.

In the trunk she folds the evening dress,
kids' clothes, sealed papers. Edible
the little fruits and gingerbread dragons.

On the landing the trunk turns out to be lined
with striped silk. Emptiness, odour of lavender.
Yesterday swans swam here like ships.

The words stumble. Stories
turn to babble. The kids'
names get forgotten.

There was a forest with grey trunks,
a big animal that she watched
with detachment. Beast, she'd think, beast.

Wind blows a song in fifths
and octaves. Stretched branches wave
the last of their hands. There's a boat

to take her out of the empty harbour.
Her voice is still audible. She's not yet
boarding for the silent feast.

2

This is here, you think, this is now.
Dry weeds, bear's breech dead
by the asphalt. Desirous of place

you read the sky as a map.
You feel the hours. Midnight,
winter? It's now, it's here.

Snow had fallen, roof tiles
showed shadowy grey through white, you could hear
sparrows' beaks tapping on stone.

The boy on the platform, you see
the bag by his shoes, how he moves
his shoulders, yawns, eats.

Till the train squeals past concrete,
the wind's pull fondles his hair. You think
a station in Germany, is it this late

you think. It's all happening in grey convolutions
hissing beneath your skull. All,
all of it: the watery course of the tracks,

the stalks bled dry, tolling bells,
fireworks, the boy. It's nothing,
a quivering cell wall, explosion, nothing.

3
Just the way we own the words
we have house, garden and children,
moving over for new takers.

What's left of us is a footprint in the ground,
a kiss on a child's cheek. We're supposed to make
lips freeze, eyes light up.

We shepherd the brain, proudly balance a trough
of memory on our necks. Treasures
we lug toward a horizon in ignorance.

How careful we are. The way we watch out
again this year: not to fall, not
to subside, not scream, not yet.

trans. Lloyd Haft

River

So often I have sought in the vicinity of rivers
for proof it was possible; I run into myself
at times mating in tall grass, hear water, wind –
swans flying over measuring unborn time
with wooden wings; the copulation rhythm says
black-white, yes-no, so does your heart and that's
it, a lap is it, is forever

At bad times I sought treacherously half-heartedly
the opposite: how I could let myself slide
breasts cunt and all into that murmuring black mother,
rocked in poisonous embrace done comfortingly away with.
How would I lie then, blue and swollen among
reed stalks, terror of the moorhens? oh no

A strange compromise occurred in
the clear winter night when I, at ten o'clock
or thereabouts, girded myself with skates
and slid forth, forth over black ice with an occasional
silver fish mounted in it, made real haste
for never again, for nowhere

trans. Lloyd Haft

LEONARD NOLENS

Poetry

Sleeping birds dream.
And sleeping birds learn as they dream to sing.
Thrushes, canaries and blackbirds, they doze
Without sexual frustrations,
Without superegos they doze off tonight
When they think, think with head and tail
Of songs, dream with heart and soul
Of songs, songs, songs
That they'll sing tomorrow, tomorrow, tomorrow.

The brains of sleeping zebra finches, they store
The staves of their colleagues
In the nucleus robustus archistriatalis.
The nucleus robustus archistriatalis tonight plays
Back the tunes they heard from nephews and nieces
By day, they dream to freshen up the fifths
That they learned yesterday.
The house sparrow too eavesdrops on its brothers
So its song doesn't rust.

trans. Paul Vincent

Conversation with Myself

'To sing compactly, pitch-black casually
As the blackbird does, is not the modern thing.
I loosen its fool's gold beak from my ears
And scour the wood for an elementary way
Of thinking and going. God too's always in the air.'

'Transform your flesh now into ferns and grass, hide
Your poverty in the clock gold of autumn.
Lie down under the last windows of October,
Without address, with your warm coat of lyrics,
And become the rightful owner of your futility.'

'Only now, in the steaming wood, where a breeze of odours
Tells me something old, something difficult, fine and banal
Like the world history of lovers' pain,
Only here do I become king of all my dèbacles
And also the creator of my daily doom.

trans. Paul Vincent

The Busker

The fat man's there again. My wife hangs over the sill
To watch his clambering baritone.
His head voice is the district housepainter
And in his squeeze-box the town's savings swell.
Oh, every day he elects himself mayor
Of our hearts, his career makes me green as hell.

He has earned his own hard money singing.
No one can resist his throat, his gullet.
His big mouth is daily bread, his whole life
is a basket of songs that's woven wherever he goes.
His hunger is a long street strewn with coins.

Men slow their steps. Their listening bakes his bread.
With their delight he'll buy today some summer trousers.
My wife is quiet. He climbs slowly till he's naked
Into her hearing, and his absence will never go away.
A girl lifts up her skirt and tapdances to my text.

trans. Paul Vincent

Passer-By

Excuse me, sir,
Can I have a light?
And do you
Know the way home?

I ask you this as a son looking up with a neck ache
At an abyss where his parents sleep in him.

Stand still for a
Moment, sir.
I'm not used to
The street any more

When you turn away from my smoking figure.
Shake hands with this cloud or I'm just air.

Today, dear sir
Not an hour,
Not a person passed
Without my disappearing

From my sight, don't let me go! And talk to me!
I am a kite on the line of your voice.

trans. Paul Vincent

Travel

Travel, oh, I've found other ways here
Of making myself invisible and thrown my house far away.
Long fasting for instance is a greedy way
Of finding the location of a cloud,
And a short, stiff drinking bout is a calming landscape.
Travel, oh, I've found other ways here.

My words for example, they are scarcely cold
When yours take me off to another world.
Yes, it is often the one where we say goodbye,
But that constant leaving too is a fixed place.
I so love sitting here at that table by the window
Eating the distance where you now live with my eyes.

(In Memoriam Herman de Coninck, 1944-1997)

trans. Paul Vincent

Albatross

That travel, those journeys of yours the last few years,
All alibis for an inveterate albatross
To fly yourself to sleep henceforth, all
Excuses high in seventh heaven, all
Poor excuses so as never to land any more
On your feet, never again wobbling from your desk

To your bed.

You became calm from that turbulent atlas in your head,
Serene from places that your tears could not yet see.
Your thirst for adventure? Curious sorrow,
Forced up from the chair of a reading boy.
What did you read? 'Look, I land in a street.
And slowly and silently my wings close

In a woman.'

(In Memoriam Herman de Coninck, 1944-1997)

Numbered

A sudden death is called in French
Une mort de poète.
But every death is sudden.

Only the dying,
Dying alone lasts long.
No, death lasts longer than dying.

My days are numbered.
Yours are not.

(In Memoriam Herman de Coninck, 1944-1997)

trans. Paul Vincent

Epitaph

I have a love who's as old as myself.
She cannot die as long as I'm not dead.

She so likes being burdened by my name.
She publishes my flesh and blood till it's all gone.

She hawks outdated news of me around the world
And blindly sorts the lines I never understood.

I have a love, she's always in danger
And can only leave when I don't know the way.

The road that we are on, we roll it slowly up
Into a stone. We'll lay it one day on our grave.

trans. Paul Vincent

Newcomer

The way was long. Your doors remain tight shut.
I am forbidden. I'm not allowed inside.
I'm not art. I'm barred from your great church.
Though I'm related to your canon.

But I understand, hunger on worn-out shoes
Doesn't make a Van Gogh, and my weary gait
Isn't a nocturne by Chopin, the sweaty smell
Of my square figure is not a Loos.

The latch is stuck. The door key is broken.
An tomorrow I'll be fifty, a fleshy conversation
With Missenburg – no Dante to show me how.
No you, no science fiction to emulate me.

For fifty years, Rimbaud, I haven't died.
For fifty years I've survived my death.
I'm still right there at hand, ready to pick up.
It's not possible not to be myself.

The way is long. Your doors remain tight shut.
Though I'm related to your dog.
I do not write that down to cut a caper.
I have no style, no pain left made of paper.

trans. Paul Vincent

I

Today five billion people said I
With a kiss, a razor blade, a plate of spaghetti, a shot.
It made a difference to me. It made me five billion times I.
We call that reality. It has no name.

Last night five billion people cried you
In letters, in the street, in pubs, in beds, on bridges.
It made a difference to me. It made me five billion.
We call that world. The world. It has no name.

But I am it. I'm it five billion times.
The world is always five billion times I.
Reality is always five billion.
Today five billion people said me.

HANS R. VLEK

The Canto of Petrus Romerus
... 61 AD ...
for M

As a retired Octavian I managed to procure
    a little villa near Cartagena,
after long struggles with the refined Gaul and raw Celt.
There at sunset I enjoy a vitamin-rich cena,*
not impecunious, careful with the copper coins in my money belt.

On my patio I rest by roses and a terracotta beaker
– a present from a tribune whose title escaped my mind –
and write verses, of beauty to be sure,
like that fool Tertsarus in his bath of suicide –

If my quintet is a success, then I stew a little tuna
in the juice of olives and herbs, pinch a little sea-salt in.
Afterwards of course my beaker of heavily-watered wine,
and add an ounce of almonds and the cactus fig.

Balba once brought my scrolls to Capri Tiberius',
but he swore by Vergilius's peasant doggerel rhyme.
I go out wandering in the evening now in a plebeian toga,
concealed my song of the impure gold sestertius!

*Spanish late-evening meal

                      trans. P.C. Evans

Long-stay

The ladies in the pavilion stare quietly out,
dozing with heads full of medicines on their chairs.
They could sit for weeks so to wilt, day
in day out, flowers try their best, but with no success.

They go silent and sleeping and without complaint
to their hell of sorrow and eternally missed chances. They
have never understood anything of life, never known love.
Compassion helps as little as a roll of chocolate buttons.

If I were christ or buddha and said: 'Come
grey daughters, even sunlight is intelligence, laugh
over a book or dive into the arts like a bath': they
would sit staring still by a beaker of cold coffee.

Their luke-warm lethargy goes to breakfast in the morning
and in the evening to the clinic's beds, prepared for nothing.

That Monotheistic Religion

The old lady on the train is reading Freud, there
Sigmund proposes that no god spoke to Moses:
how lonely she must be as she sits to stare
out of the window, with her father complex, her projection
and the featureless
view, as un-elevated as an overly long poem is,

between old Groningen and older Maastricht, whilst
wondrous clouds and small-spired villages
pass by in a Golden Age museum light –
the fertile meadows beside the Holland Railway Line are
more fruitful than Arcady, and it has

to be these good grounds here:
the grassy meadows where the Lord goes,
where one with naïve beliefs industriously hoes,
and looks up to that pupil of Charcot, out of the back of whose
head such amazing bovine extrapolation flows –

trans. P.C. Evans

Geranium

From the poorly-sitting
school bench, in an odour of dust,
old wood and piss, beneath high windows
in a blistering frame: the red
of the geranium.

My grandmother toiling over
a tub in the garden, and alongside
a tidy tiled path in a row, in the red
about which my grandpa spoke
in committee: geraniums.

At home we had one
which would never bloom
as everyone stubbed their butts out
in the pot, O god the dejection
of that hairy-green, knobbly
stem!

Geranium, wonderful bloom
that is not beautiful,
wine of the grocer, chicken
among birds, jewel
for everything that is poor and cheap.

The Sonnet of Angel Pasquelito, Manilla

No dinero. No money. Every day I go before dark
with my younger brother to the rubbish heap.
There we find rotten grapefruits, left-overs
of city restaurants and sometimes, for me, little tart,

an old nylon stocking. Sometimes little, sometimes barely
enough. My brother carries the plastic bag, then
I bring him home again, still early. Father has ulcers,
mother is bearing the seventh child beneath our candle and cross.

Then it's quick, quick a pair of the old nylons on and with
darkness to the busy city centre full of lights and halls of assembly.
There Jesus grants to me dispensation to suck-off a tourist or a
            gringo
from the army camp, enough to pay for fresh fish and oil for the
            lamp

for a week or more. Our country is the most beautiful upon earth.
You should see the moon above the morning hills just glow! I am
thirteen now.

trans. P.C. Evans

The Ballad of the Beast

Bernd and Bertha, both busy
buffing up and brushing the brothel:
Bernd buffs the brown bar, Bertha
brushes off the blue velvet blinds –

Bernd and Bertha, both from Bremen,
bent brushing above the brown and blue;
Boss Bolle, after bestial bacchanal, still in bed.
Above the bar bells and beakers of Babelsbräu.

Bernd brings balloons of blubber to the bin
by the blow bench, built in Boston,
where boss bought it with billiards.
Bertha blankets the brown breasts

of the bizarre bust on the bronze beer
taps with bleach: built in baroque style on the bar.
Boss the bulbous billionaire burps in bed,
Bertha obliging the blow-up bunnies still greased –

Bernd buffs off the board: 'with the best beverage
we bring you bare buttocks' and blows
a gob upon his brush for the better brilliance.
Bertha buries bins full of blubber balloons

outside at the back: 'Broommm!' An emblazoned bike
brings bright brochures to the burghers in the suburbs.
And baby blue above the boulevard beams
the bawn. Bernd bawls for Bertha

to come back in and both of them buff the bar and the brothel
brown and blue and barnyard beaming.
Bernd bolts up the stairs with the bubble bath
and then the Bordeaux-bedecked bestial alcoves.

Both beings being all but done with the bizniz,
but for the bearing of boss 'beefbreastbuttock' to the bar,

the brothel is ready for business. Bernd and Bertha,
both abysmally imbursed, disembark from the brothel
with bliss. Broken by buffing and bending
they beat their way to the bus stop on the boulevard.

And baby blue beams the bawn –

trans. P.C. Evans

The Hydrocyanic Blues
for M

I am Abraham Weinstock, your servant,
once through Belsen's chimney, I would rise high.
As museum director I spread refinement,
now by Jehovah's battlements I rest and abide –

My love for my fellow man was never understood truly,
my black felt-hat always boundlessly despised.
My heart, through seven languages, as a moonstone borne with me,
found its strength on Sinai, where my waiting shadow lies.

My daughter was a thorn in Goebbels' eye,
her nose too eastern, her Greek too perfect.
For her, Wagner and Nietzsche would have stood aside,
if Arminius had not granted a corporal a ready wit –

But above the earth our life is better:
in Ravensbrück, my Romanian spouse was murdered,
now we rest peacefully in transcendental ether:
our hora is forgotten and our tongue disturbed –

The Sestertius of Faustina Junior

The hairstyle of Annia Galeria Faustina
is extremely elegant, locks bound up into a knot.
Every morning she stood before a bronze mirror,
combing it up neatly into a wreath.

In 145, she married Marcus Aurelius, who
with full beard laurelled, allowed himself continually to be coined.
She too was permitted upon the sestertius, a fine
penny that laid a plebeian girl flat on her back.

But of this Annia Galeria had little understanding,
dispatching fruit and foul she divided
the imperial couch and saw her hairstyle made thus
known become the fashion in the whole of the empire.

An elegant look for a weekend at the gladiators';
a charming smile for an emasculated slave.

trans. P.C. Evans

A Short History of Lust
...esse delendam.

Mithras had forbidden unto Mani the dewy grape,
even Augustinus, with Hippo, defended the law –
the buttocked peach was only for the gods to take,
and the asparagus, dear ladies, ask of it no more...

Fellatio and Cunnilingus, clowns from Ostia, south of Rome,
went roving merry the flat globe round,
Cunnilingus with a peach, and the good Fellatio
with a creamy asparagus in his painted mouth -

Hippo went to ruin on the old Carthaginian shore,
for an old Carthaginian shore is the best,
like Tanit and Dido. And lastly, to rest,
there's been nothing since then but lust and more
lust and luxuria, three gilded ells high. And Vi
behind a window, humming as her money multiplies –

EVA GERLACH

Vocabulary

This is your eyeball. This the sun. This cold
that tugs at you, is draught through the open window.
This water, where you will always fit in.

That is the kettle, that sings on the fire,
above the four knobs that turn on the gas.
That is the bread knife, plunged into the breadboard.

All of these things you must remember well.
Today or tomorrow they will have their way.

trans. P.C. Evans

Pressure

It is strange the way it is with the dead,
sidling up to you, sitting with their
sockets in your knees, their digits
in your fingers, writing a letter,
just as sluggish as you, just as unclear about the latest
on the weather report and mercy, doubt and cost price

and when it's dinner time, bedtime,
time to let out the dog,
time to bear a child, or bury a man,
always they walk, meekly,
obediently, with their combs and their thorns their pelvic bone
over your genitals their skull around your
senses their spine around your marrow

running all through you, tickticktick. Your skin alone
dampens their pressure a little.

(Metro) Journey

He enters (Van der Madeweg) and sits down
that thing won't leave him be he sits tapping rapping
smacks his lips then rhymes something.

Here alongside him in the order of the day
you see 1 ear without a ring in the opposite order
rides 1 with a ring from behind
you see how on his head he has two ears
that jerk back from the front you know that his nose has done that.

He gives himself over entirely to the execution
of what now moves him 'a hair's breadth'
shoots him past the stadium shoots him
right through his heart 'real tough man'. He slumps

trans. P.C. Evans

Doppelgänger

A man who cycled so hard that we nearly didn't see him
passed by and called with a rough voice look out.
But before we could do anything he was already gone
and before we could look at him he was a distance away.

He must have been a professional if you saw how he
disappeared beneath the viaduct, almost transparent, a cloud
of dust, not that that blew up from the asphalt but he himself
growing thinner and thinner from forever reeling himself in.

Crumb

We can't see what is whole, it is
too big, doesn't befit us or fit
in our heads
but what's diced, minced, finely ground,
crumbled, blended, atomised, decayed –

All that's divided is in us for good.

trans. Paul Vincent

What is lost
For L

Map in your head. A house,
light switches, doors leading in or out, steps
so many upstairs or down, four
points of the stove.

Map of a body that is dressed or not
of such and such a length and width,
open under this name, in which you fit

till you no longer inhabit it. How did the cupboards go,
where on earth my scars.

New ones on top. The crashing, banging,
grabbing and missing, the difference
between one to a million and life-size

of things when they are no longer called
what. When no memory clothes them.

Illuminating all things

Sol qui illustras omnia solus
    Bruno, *Cantus Circaeus*

What was it that you said, something about pike
early that winter morning when the dark
cloaked you and your father singly
on the moped, each cut their ice-hole
and you casting with the what's-it rod,
such-and-such a hook, tiddly
bait from the bucket: never catching
one pike. Wasn't there a lamp,
didn't we have it later, that standing type,
blotchy metal, hangable too.

Keeping everything in mind,
all things, time and place, substance, quan-
tity and quality. Being
a god that moves it.
            Sometimes you saw one
unmoving in the depths, with that pointed
snout of theirs, grey patches.

trans. Paul Vincent

But What of the Ant

I said to someone
Don't think it will pass,
that if you leave or drop dead,
the grass will just come up,
the magpie just take the prunings again
in its mouth, build a nest,
it's not as easy as that.

No. When you're no longer there,
when I no longer have your wakefulness
and your sleepfulness, it will
all go wrong. Because there'll be
no more reason for things
to exist.

And someone began to laugh,
what's wrong, he said, do you still want to
arrive somewhere, do you still think
that in presence a truth resides
greater than just that
of the address?

But what of the ant, I cried, its running
across the ground, the way it
lifts sand grains and eggs,
builds its nest under the plant and its fruit
and the root that grows in the sand.

Someone wrote his name on
me right over mine, someone buried himself
in me where I did not know
I was.
Then he escaped, and then

he vanished from sight and I stood in the light,
burst all white from my bark and spread my branches.

trans. Paul Vincent   169

Often quite horizontal

A thrush: we'd never had one
in all those ten years, sang in the elder and sang
under our window just as we'd imagined
they sang. And sat with its beak full of beetles
still whenever we looked, for whole evenings
we ate hunched, we couldn't get enough
till, *would you say cheep? No, chook*, it stayed away.
For a while I tried its song
for early morning, four-line ample
verses with something regal and something
of scrabbling in the earth but it was no good, all along
what I had not heard and had not missed
began to nag faintly. Why
if you forget so much of what you see, let go
so soon – you won't catch me – of things
that you wonder if you exist, does the lightest
thing always come past, wait till the coast is clear,
call you with beaks full of food.

trans. Paul Vincent

ESTHER JANSMA

Under the Old Eyes of the Night

Torches, it was hot,
people danced, smoke drifted
like oil between their pale faces,
an old man yelled, and so on.

Among us stood the snow queen.
I knew who she was by her frail shoulders
and her wings like knives and the look
in her eyes melting like ice from within.
When she saw me, she broke
into a laugh that was warm.

No one looked while she melted.
A woman in small red boots stepped
into the puddle, and cursed. I smacked her.
I bent over and drank from the asphalt
what I suddenly loved. I tell you,

I knelt like a lover.
Before you, with your drunken face, fell over me,
sailor, this pier was a bridal bed.

trans. Mark Strand

Epilogue

My daughter is grown. She has no face.
Under her brows she is a mirror.
I gaze into her and think: 'How beautiful!'
My fingers leave smudges behind.

Between her neck and the collar of her coat
water wells up. Water drips from her wrists.
'Are you crying?' I ask. 'Does crying go like this
if you've got no eyes?' She does not reply.

'I wish you would exist,' I say.
She falls and pulls up her knees, shrinks
until a child is lying there,
and the absence of child.

I lift her up. Shattered glass: crick, crack.
We are a silhouette, and disappearing.

Dolores' Wish

I lived in a cauldron on the beach.
Each morning I'd throw open the lid
and turn into sand, salt, sun
and into dead fish with white teeth.

A prince appeared. His shadow reached
into the farthest corners of my house, glittering
with mica. He said: 'How cramped you live.'
The sea continued making wide sounds of sea,
seagulls screamed.

I narrowed my eyes, peered
at his neck, its perfect skin
disappearing shamelessly under a white shirt,
and fell in love. I answered: 'Yes.'

Now, I am only Dolores
from the slums of El Colorado
on the Gulf of California.

Fish, Talking Fish, take Dolores the Pauper
out of me.

trans. Steve Orlen

Florence

Beneath our balcony, a tongue
in the dusty mouth of the city,
blond tourists with children's faces
stand stunned in the wake of the sun.
The evening rattles with cutlery.

We look for a square
where a thousand strangers
are the centre, the eye,
by sun and sex rubbed to shine,
drink wine and wine
until, flapping our fins, we capsize
and, dancing like dust
in the throat of Florence,
get lost.

trans. Steve Orlen

Papier Mâché

I am the big recycling machine.
The rags my father turned into,
those wisps of sound from mouths grown old,
I chew to pulp.

As long as I smoke cigarettes
he will smell of tobacco on my hand,
as long as I am scared of death
he will be too.

He is my doll, I play with him
whenever. Worrying,
he kisses away the scratches on my knees,
but doesn't say much.

trans. Steve Orlen

Transportation

The girl sits in the kitchen
and plays with the hairy
wrist of a gentleman
who is sitting on an airplane to Cairo.
What a beautiful watch!

The girl lies on her belly
in her garden of poisonous green polyester
and listens to the birds
in the voice of a gentleman who orders a cocktail
on the airplane to Rome.
What Italian words!

The girl stands in front of the mirror
and paints her lips
and looks at the lady
who smiles at the gentleman on the airplane to Cuba...

the girl lies in bed.
She closes her eyes.
She holds in her belly.
These are not her hands.

Archaeology

If, then, we have to clothe ourselves,
against the cold, for instance, or in the name of something,
in the shreds of this or that time past,
stories and memory-props that tell us nothing

except that we were already there
in the today that existed before today –
if we can only preserve ourselves in the now
by continually re-inventing ourselves in the now,

then preferably simply by means of clothing.
You are sitting at table. Suddenly you see how someone
was crossing ice, how the cold got its grip on him

or some other fate and you say: look,
here you have his shoes, leather jacket, gloves.
Where is time? Time is here.

trans. James Brockway

The Lovers

He lay washed up on red rocks
and dreamed her voice was calling him, sand
scattered over him and blowing away.

The sea lay itself down on his breast.
His heart was the breeding-ground of
colourful birds. The wind came back.

One by one the birds rose up,
they shrieked and fell upwards, helpless,
they were swept aside.

When she found him his heart was a wound,
a deserted chamber, the difference between him
and the ground was love, no more.

She lifted him up. Gently she tried
to close his lips. In the ship
she tried to close his mouth.

She grew silent and pressed his lips together.
She grew silent and laid his arms round her neck.
It worked. His head lies on her shoulder.

He is silent. They set sail. They are everything
to each other.

trans. James Brockway

Concerning the Writing of Beautiful Nature Poems

Writing nature poems is a complicated business,
something to think long about, sigh over,
in Dutch, for instance, about 'boom' and 'rood', how they differ.
How to remove the difference. Processes, you think,

how water dissolves ink, something of that kind -
but how does a 'boom' make its way to 'rood'?
Does dying light suggest itself? Reject it.
Someone hanging from a bough, bleeding? Winter,

and in it, a robin? And more of that sort. Nothing
fits the bill. Then: you dismiss the 'b' at the beginning,
and the sealing-off the 'm', treat the 'r' as disposable, say

that 'd' is dead, and you are left with: two times 'oo'.
Not beautiful, pretty bare, an almost helpless 'o, o!'
Writing nature poems is demolition work.

trans. James Brockway

Descent

We crossed the Styx.
The ferryman lay drunk in his boat.
I took the helm and we sank like stones.

Water like the earth consists of layers,
transparent ribbons, glistening strata
of ever less life, less warmth.

Bubbles blossomed in your hair,
the current tugged your head backwards
and caressed your throat.

Stones waved with algae and ferns,
gurgled softly, sang of 'peace'.
They sliced your clothes away.

Fish licked the blood from your legs.
I held your hand tight. I wanted to comfort you,
but we were falling too fast and no words can exist

without air; my love
lay above, blue balloons, brief buoys,
marking the site of the accident,

before flowing on. Your mouth fell open,
your face turned red, your two hands sought
for balance, sought my arms.

You tried to climb up inside me.
You were a glass blower with a cloud of diamonds
circling his mouth. I hugged you like a kitten.

I stroked your fingers.
You held on tight.
You fell asleep. I stroked your fingers, let go.

trans. James Brockway

K. MICHEL

—

I draw back the curtains
in the distance a river flows
gleaming in the morning light
a deeply laden barge draws
a v-shaped trail

I clear the table
the flowers in the slender vase
are question marks, the radio
presents a survey of the facts

I sit down and stare
at the grain in the tabletop

the sand smells musty
the light casts long
shadows across the field
there's a rustling in the shrubs

I put a house on the table
the shutters are a yellow-white check
smoke curls up the chimney

hello, anybody home
I call to the house
fear not, I am just
an animal in search of shelter

the wind pushes the door shut

a flock of wood pigeons flies
up flapping, finches
shoot out on all sides

the house solidifies into a wall

I turn around and see the magical lights
dancing between the trees

I trip over a molehill
a startled pheasant crosses the path
branches strike me in the face

before I reach the clearing near
the lake, I am called back

travel news, a jam on the A3
a man speaks of a woman
'with a huge pair of headlights'

where am I, where was I
the flowers give no hint

When she awakes

The first thing she thinks
when she awakes is
I'm flying, I am in heaven

Through the blue haze
she sees a cloud and
she hears birds singing

She gets to her feet and takes
a few steps that sound hollow
but the blue haze is so strong
that she has to sit down

Slowly it is dawning on her
that she is at the bottom
of a pumped out swimming pool

Her head is thumping
her hands are sticky
she wants a drink of water
a soluble aspirin

It must have been a wild night
but she doesn't remember a thing

Sure, Chinese lanterns in the trees
a salsa band on the steps
In her ears a dull noise is ringing

'They're all bastards'

She slumps down lazily and lies
stretched out on her back
and lets herself float on the light

trans. William Groenewegen

Are frogs the canaries

Not just in polluted areas
but also in reserves like Yosemite Park
frogs are dying out world-wide

Is it the hole in the ozone layer
Are pesticides in the atmosphere to blame

Frogs have a permeable skin
and where water and air deteriorate
they are among the first animals to vanish

(Above the tower blocks I see a plane
dragging a fuse behind it that slowly
burns up in the rusty evening sky

And I smell the ditch in Leijpark
thirty years ago, the pearly spawn
between my fingers, the brownish odour
of tadpoles caught with Ivo
in the zinc tub at the back of the garden)

In the bar and the corridors of this first
global conference experts ask themselves
are frogs the canaries in our coalmine

trans. William Groenewegen

—

Great river! Turn round!
Flow back to the mountains
Don't trust the lowland, the towns.
Here evil reigns supreme
Here every corner is cut off.

The wind is ochre and stifling
The rate dominates it all
And the fields are green with poison.

Turn round! Take them along!
I play the accordion
I can read the map.

We'll go beyond the tree line
I will build a hut.
We'll listen to the silence
We'll praise the air.
And at night we'll count the satellites.

No time to lose.
Avanti comrade!

We'll forget the banners
The grand words, the wind band
for yesterday has gone.
We won't think of profit or loss.
We'll see about the future later.

trans. William Groenewegen

Under the stars

This morning I awoke
with a terrible word on the tip of my tongue
A sledgehammer blow. An ice age
A brief sound given me to destroy all others

Finito! The babbling
the judging and debating
No more editorials, no speeches, no news-at-ten
Exit the tiresome standing around at parties and receptions
Gratifying calm at the stock exchange
The world will bask in an unrealistic bright light

The responsibility weighs heavily on my shoulders
The possible disappearance of all music
The rising of sexual tension through the sudden silence
All those sports addicts without commentary
All those lost commuters, not a train will leave on time
Everyone will suddenly be a world citizen and alien everywhere

Will I myself be touched
or will I be the only one to continue living in the way of words
in a solitude, now unimaginable,
cut off from my friends and family who, like before
the fall, will move very differently through the world

Can I bear it? Can I oversee the consequences of this deed?
Why have I been chosen, me, a simple poet
Is this the beginning of the end, must I spend
the rest of my life in this uncertain night
afraid to fall asleep, afraid to speak in dreams
waiting for the morning, waiting for a sign
waiting for a decision

(–)

call it a curtain of mirrors
call it a blind wall for all I care

at least something
that surrounds us

something that must be unsettled or unhinged
broken open for perspective to

for the world between the words
in all its multiplicity

for the things between the words
in all their simplicity

not to be read
but to be seen

to be seen without
a b c in between

trans. William Groenewegen

Rule of Thumb

If the house is infected, they said
in the village of my grandparents
then lock up a pig for the night
the evil will crawl into the beast
and next morning all will be clean

In the structure that every life is
there comes a time called
being in deep water, a leak
has covered the walls in Rorschach figures
and it smells of something that once
was hidden during an old game

Look round the table and try
to find out who's left holding the baby
which is a hot tip for poker players
if you don't spot the victim
then there's only one option left

So I say this new day
to the face in the shaving mirror
stop digging if you're in a rut
be prepared to say ow & yes
look around you, search all the rooms
and if you don't find the pig
then it must be you

The hands in the girl

When she was little
her mother sailed into the hereafter
like a boomerang

to pop up night after night
in this severe winter
and its crunching cold

She sits straight up in bed
stares at the shadows on the wall
and claps her hands

then she walks down the stairs to the kitchen
and scoffs everything in the fridge

It is a presence she cannot
grasp, cannot embrace
a stiffening that slowly
freezes up her spine

During her lunch break she sits nauseous
in a corner, turned away from the others
and looks at the man in the square
who stands there in the silty snow
blue with cold selling roast chestnuts

Raised in the ways of the Old Testament
she has the firm belief she is paying
for the bikini days of summer

Once home she entrenches herself
with the phone in front of the television
and calls all her friends
Round midnight she arms herself
with white wine and fashion mags

Later in the kitchen the feeling
creeps up on her that they're not her
hands but her mother's that
empty out the fridge through her body

Exhausted by throwing up she falls asleep
with a pillow clenched to her breast
while she softly mutters 'mermaid'

(一)

Golden fish!
Turn heaven upside down!

Light up the city, the harbour.
Let the windows shine.
Colour the quay
the gloomy boats ruby, the tall cranes.
Haul the day above water.

The lighthouse waits.
The statue of Colun waits.
The market of San José. The seagulls.
The broad streets lined with plane trees.

The light red of dreams.
The darkness of unrest.
The light blue of desire.

The horizon waits.
The passengers that approach,
Linda. The early wind.
The taxis by the pier. Customs.
The walls of this hotel room.

Jump
Great golden fish. Jump!

trans. William Groenewegen

THE POETS

H. H. ter Balkt (1938) has published eighteen collections since 1969. He won the Henriette Roland Holst Prize for *Waar de burchten stonden en de snoek zwom* (1980), and the Jan Campert Prize for *Aardes deuren* (1987). His collected work *In de water-wingebieden* was published in 2000.

Remco Campert (1929) is the most sober of the experimentalist generation of the 1950's. He has published numerous poetry collections, novels and short stories. He writes for the national newspaper *de Volkskrant*. His awards include the Jan Campert Prize (1956) and the P.C. Hooft Prize (1979).

Hugo Claus (Belgium, 1929) is perhaps the most important living author in the Dutch language area. He moved to Paris in 1947, where he met Antonin Artaud. He also came into contact there with the experimentalist Dutch writers of the 1950's. His first novel was published in 1950, his first collection of poems in 1954. His masterpiece *The Sorrow of Belgium* appeared in 1983. He has won more prizes than any other Dutch writer.

J. Eijkelboom (1926) has published seven collections and is the principle translator of English-language poetry into Dutch. His *Collected Poems* will appear in the summer of 2002.

Anna Enquist (1945) has published five collections and a *Collected Poems*. She made a stormy entrance into Dutch literature in 1991 with *Soldatenliederen*, which immediately won the C. Buddingh Prize. She has also published two novels *Het meesterstuk* (1994) and *Het Geheim* (1997).

Eva Gerlach (1948) published her first collection in 1979; nine more followed. Her *Selected Poems* appeared in 1999. She has won the Jan Campert Prize (1995) and the P.C. Hooft Prize (2000). She is also an acclaimed children's author.

Judith Herzberg (1934) has published poetry, plays, translations and film scripts. She is one of Holland's most widely-read poets and has been translated into English, German and Turkish. She was awarded the P.C. Hooft Prize for her oeuvre in 1997.

Esther Jansma (1958) works as an archeologist. She has published five collections. She won the VSB Prize for *Hier is de tijd* (1998). Her most recent collection is *Dakruiters* (2001).

Rutger Kopland (1934) has published thirteen collections and won every major Dutch poetry prize. A selection of his work in English translation was published by Enitharmon in 1991 and a definitive selection by Harvill in 2001.

Gerrit Kouwenaar (1923) is 'the grand old man of Dutch poetry'. He was imprisoned by the Nazis in 1943 and was a leading member of the Experimentalist Group of the 1950's. His *Collected Poems* appeared in 1982 and a new *Selected Poems* in 1998. He won the Nijhoff Prize for his translations of Brecht, Goethe and Sartre in 1967 and the Prize for Dutch Letters in 1989.

K. Michel (1958) published his first collection in 1990 *Ja, naakt als de stenen*. He won the Herman Gorter Prize in 1995 and his latest collection *Waterstudies* won the VSB Prize 2000. He is co-editor of the magazine *Raster*.

Leonard Nolens (Belgium, 1947) writes poetry and diaries. In 1998, the fourth impression of *Hart tegen hart* was published, containing all of the work published between 1975 and 1996. He received the Constantijn Huygens Prize for his oeuvre in 1997.

Willem van Toorn (1935) publishes novels and poetry. He won the Jan Campert Prize in 1982 and the Herman Gorter Prize in 1992. His *Collected Poems* appeared in January 2001, and the novel, *The River*, in 1999.

Hans R. Vlek (1947) published his first collection *Anatomy for Murderers* in 1965 at the age of eighteen. He won the Jan Campert Prize in 1968 and his first *Selected Poems* was published in 1970. A series of stunning collections began appearing in the mid 1980's combining classical and hermetic reading with formal brilliance and natural wit. He currently lives in Granada, Spain.

THE TRANSLATORS

James Brockway published many translations of Dutch prose and poetry. He won the prestigious Nijhoff Prize and was honoured with a knighthood. His translations of Rutger Kopland were published by Harvill shortly before his death in 2001.

P.C. Evans is a poet and freelance translator. His first collection, *The Unreal City*, was published by Headland in 2001.

Willem Groenewegen is a teacher and poetry translator. A collection of his translations of Arjen Duinker will be published by Arc in 2003.

Lloyd Haft teaches Chinese Literature at the University of Leiden. He has published eight collections of poetry in Dutch and English (Querido, Amsterdam).

Francis R. Jones lectures at the University of Newcastle. He has published many translations from Russian, Serbo-Croat and Dutch, including of the poets Ivan Lalic and Hans Faverey.

Shirley Kaufman is an American poet who lives in Jerusalem. Her latest collection, *Threshold*, will be published by Copper Canyon Press in 2003.

Steve Orlen has published five poetry collections, including *This Particular Eternity* (Ausable Press, 2001). He currently teaches at the University of Arizona and at Warren Wilson College.

Craig Raine is a poet, Fellow in English at New College Oxford and editor of the magazine *Areté*. His latest publication is *A la recherche du temps perdu* (Picador, 2000).

John Scott and **Graham Martin**'s selection of Remco Campert, *In the Year of the Strike*, was first published in 1968.

Mark Strand is the former Poet Laureate of the United States. He now teaches at the University of Chicago. His *Selected Poems* was published in Britain by Carcanet.

Rina Vergano, a freelance translator, lives in Bristol. She has translated many leading Dutch playwrights, as well as poetry and film scripts.

Paul Vincent was Senior Lecturer in Dutch at University College London and is now a fulltime translator. His numerous publications include translations of the novelists Harry Mulisch (Penguin) and J. Bernlef (Faber).

THE EDITORS

Rob Schouten (1954) is a poet and critic. He has published eight collections. He won the Herman Gorter Prize for his latest collection *Infauste dienstprognose* (2000). He writes for the national newspaper *Trouw*.

Robert Minhinnick (1952) lives in Porthcawl, south Wales. He edited the anthology of Welsh poetry in translation, *In Een Ander Licht* (Wagner & van Santen, 2001). His latest collection is *After the Hurricane* (Carcanet, 2002). He is the editor of *Poetry Wales*.